PENNSYLVANIA FIRESIDE TALES

VOLUME 3

JEFFREY R. FRAZIER

CATAMOUNT
PRESS

an imprint of Sunbury Press, Inc.
Mechanicsburg, PA USA

CATAMOUNT
PRESS

an imprint of Sunbury Press, Inc.
Mechanicsburg, PA USA

For information about special discounts for bulk purchases, please contact Sunbury Press Orders Dept. at (855) 338-8359 or orders@sunburypress.com.

To request one of our authors for speaking engagements or book signings, please contact Sunbury Press Publicity Dept. at publicity@sunburypress.com.

FIRST CATAMOUNT PRESS EDITION: April 2024

Set in Adobe Garamond | Interior design by Crystal Devine | Cover by Lawrence Knorr | Edited by Debra Reynolds.

Publisher's Cataloging-in-Publication Data
Names: Frazier, Jeffrey R., author.
Title: Pennsylvania fireside tales volume 3 / Jeffrey R. Frazier.
Description: First trade paperback edition. | Mechanicsburg, PA : Catamount Press, 2024.
Summary: Volume 3 in the Pennsylvania Fireside Tales series exploring the origins and foundations of old-time Pennsylvania mountain folktales, legends, and folklore.
Identifiers: ISBN : 979-8-88819-209-2 (paperback) | ISBN : 979-8-88819-210-8 (ePub).
Subjects: NATURE / Ecosystems & Habitats / Mountains | HISTORY / United States / State & Local / Middle Atlantic (DC, DE, MD, NJ, NY, PA) | FICTION / Fairy Tales, Folk Tales & Mythology.

Designed in the USA
0 1 1 2 3 5 8 13 21 34 55

For the Love of Books!

Cover: "Bull Elk" likely Edwin Henry Landseer circa 1850.

To my parents and both my grandmothers,
from whom I learned to love Pennsylvania's mountains,
and to the old-time mountain folks whose stories
form the soul of these awe-inspiring hills.

Head of the large stag shot by Samuel Strohecker in High Valley, Centre County, in 1898. (Drawing by James Frazier, from an old photograph.)

CONTENTS

Tell me a tale of the timber lands,
And the old-time pioneers;
Somethin' a poor man understands,
With his feelings as well as his ears,

Tell of the old log house –
About the loft, the puncheon floor –
The fireplace with crane swinging out
and the latchstring through the door.

From James Whitcomb Riley's "A Tale of the Airly Days"

INTRODUCTION

B ack in 1991, when I started to organize and write the episodes for the first volume in my *Pennsylvania Fireside Tales* series, I decided I could no longer afford the time it would take to travel and collect any more stories. I needed time to write if I was ever going to produce even one book, so I resolved to stop searching for the old tales in the quaint, out-of-the-way spots that seemed to keep pulling me away from my self-appointed task. However, it seems I just can't resist a good story, and whenever a promising lead came up, I chased it down. As a result, I've collected, and am still collecting, some of the best material I've found to date.

Not all the blame for my inability to stop collecting good material should fall upon the fascinating folk tales of Pennsylvania. Probably just as much fault has to be placed upon the mountains themselves. Somehow, they've always drawn me into their cool depths and shaded solitude, charming me with a seemingly endless treasure store of wonderful sights and comforting breezes. Whenever I need to feel at peace with myself or the world, or whenever the pressures of the workplace or the daily grind of everyday life seem overwhelming, I can lose myself in the mountains and there feel alive once more. These grand and somber ridges will, I suspect, always be a source of strength for me, just as they have been for many others over the years.

Most lovers of these same hills would agree, I believe, that it would not be an exaggeration to say that if anyone wishes to experience one of those rare moments of true happiness that occurs in a lifetime, they should go to the mountains and search for a teller of the old tales. When sitting amidst the scenery that is woven into the heart and soul of the stories themselves, cares of this present hectic age seem to melt away, and the listener is indeed transported to another level—a finer phase of existence that everyone should be able to experience whenever they so desire. It has been this writer's privilege to feel a renewed optimism each time I've gone back to the hills, and that's the same high that I hope the reader gets when he peruses the stories preserved in my Pennsylvania Fireside Tales and my Pennsylvania Landmarks series published by Sunbury Press.

Many folks have sincerely told me how much they've enjoyed the anecdotes I've brought to the attention of the general public, and others have even thanked me for doing so. I've always thought that these episodes deserve more publicity than they've gotten in the past, and positive comments from many kind readers have reinforced that belief. Certainly, folklorists and scholars in related fields have collected these types of tales over the years, but the results of their efforts usually don't get widely disseminated.

It would seem the scholars' main objective is to dissect, categorize, and hoard the stories for their enjoyment, seemingly often looking down with disdain upon anyone else who dares to consider folktales as property of the folk from whom they originated in the first place. Call it a popularizer versus protectionist philosophy, but, to me, once a folktale has been cast into an ivory tower of learning and placed upon some dry page of a scholar's notebook, it loses its charm and its attraction for the average person, becoming a desiccated and lifeless object.

That's not to say, on the other hand, that a legend or folktale should be meddled with in any way by the non-scholar once he's collected it. These survivors of an earlier time should not be embellished, polished, or trifled with if their purity is to be maintained; their window on the past remains unclouded. It is this approach that I've tried to take in deciding how to preserve the annals in the Fireside Tales and Mountain Landmarks volumes. I've also tried to maintain the same care when discussing the history behind the tales, but actions do fall short of intentions at times, despite the best attempts to insure otherwise.

I was rudely reminded of that fact one afternoon one year when I was having a book signing at Homan's Store in Potters Mills, Centre County.

Located at the entrance to the Seven Mountains country of Mifflin and Centre Counties, the little store is a unique throwback to an earlier and less-hurried time, and it is also a favorite stopping place for hunters and hikers who need to stock up on groceries or refuel their trucks before driving off onto one of the many dirt mountain roads nearby.

I always enjoy the atmosphere of the quaint store, but on that particular afternoon during the book signing, I was enjoying it even more. In talking to the many people who stopped by to have their books autographed, I signed a book for one young gentleman who then asked me where I had gotten the name "Henry Pickett" as the name of the Confederate general who, in my story called "Sounds of Battle" in my first volume, I cited as the leader of the infamous charge at Gettysburg. Right away, I knew I was in trouble.

I looked at the story, and sure enough, I had misnamed General George E. Pickett, whose name is forever linked to Pickett's Charge—the turning point of the Battle of Gettysburg. Since I knew his correct name, the misnomer had been a slip of the pen, but such mistakes cast doubt on the other historical facts I've tried to weave into the stories, and that's not something I want to happen.

Even though I'm not trained as a historian, I know something about research methodology, so I do try to avoid mistakes, and also note when my sources of information may be suspect. Time, however, is always an enemy of accuracy, particularly when you can't devote as much effort as you'd like into researching facts or when you're trying to write after a particularly tiring day at the office.

This dilemma was brought to my attention once again one day when doing another book signing where a woman told me her parents live in the Scotia Barrens near State College. She went on to say they live near the flat stone marking the gravesite of Bert Dilige, the infamous murderer whose story, "The Black Ghost of Scotia," appears in my Volume II of the same name. In that story, I mention that the flat stone marking the gravesite is no longer there. I did not have the time to verify this fact but instead relied upon statements in a newspaper article written some twenty years ago.

It is indeed unfortunate that I didn't, and don't, have the proper time to devote to this activity because it certainly cries out for attention. I'd like nothing better than just to collect and write these tales, but no one else seems to have the same enthusiasm, or time, for that matter, and so I continue to do so, imperfect as the results may be now and then.

I can only ask the reader to overlook the faults and enjoy the annals, promising to be as historically accurate as possible in all future efforts. Hopefully, the results, though not of the quality that scholars would demand, will still take you to that higher phase where you, too, can forget your cares and savor the finer aspects of our Pennsylvania mountains, the majestic peaks that some would say are among the Creator's most masterful works.

NOTE TO CURRENT EDITION: The preceding paragraphs are what appeared in the first edition of this volume, and the chapters that appear in this new edition are the same ones that were included in the first edition. However, although there are no new chapters in this new Sunbury Press edition, there are, as in previous editions, new photos and new information added to the original chapters.

These extras include interesting details that were not discovered until after previous editions were published and which I felt needed to be added to the chapters in order to enhance their quality. This edition also includes many new photos not included in the first edition, which add a new level of interest to the original tales.

I hope these embellishments appeal to the reader as much as they do to me. In the meantime, I continue to explore Pennsylvania's mountains. It seems they still call to me, and when they do, I must go. And that's because it's from those mountaintops that I sometimes feel that I can almost touch the "roof" of Pennsylvania, which in turn inspires me to collect still more of those old-time tales that calm the spirit but also which fire the imagination to the point where fact and romance seem one and the same.

CHAPTER 1

RED PANTHER

Pennsylvania's natural underground system of limestone caves has been described as a honeycomb of interconnecting passages and cool, subterranean streams. The most spectacular of these caverns have often been commercialized and opened to the public for tours, but numerous wild caves are sometimes even more spectacular than their commercialized counterparts, which offer just as many geological wonders and delights to weekend cave explorers.

Those spelunkers who have explored Madisonburg's Veiled Lady Cave in Centre County, for example, will remember the seemingly bottomless chasm in one of the side passages that leads to a hidden lake. A small foot log in this former commercial cave allows an explorer to cross the chasm, but the experience is not for the faint of heart.

There is also another wild cave in Centre County that provided more breathtaking excitement to a group of Boy Scouts about thirty-five years ago. Located near the town of Centre Hall, McClanahan's Cave is known for some interesting flowstone formations, but the discovery by the Scouts of a padlocked box in a side room of the cavern created momentary visions of hidden treasure, at least for a few minutes until we discovered the box was empty.

The box had no bottom either, but the thrill of the discovery will always be remembered by those of us who were there in the cave. We all speculated about what had been stored in the container in the olden times, but the old crate was probably nothing more than a remnant of the days when settlers of the area had used McClanahan's Cave for cold storage of their milk and other perishables. On the other hand, the mysterious box and its padlock reinforce the fact that both commercialized and wild caves have their unique histories and legends.

Not too far away, for example, is the famous Centre County cavern called Penn's Cave. This large commercial attraction is also known as the "all-water cavern" because the only way through it is by boat. However, Penn's Cave is also famous for its legend of Princess Nittany (for whom nearby Nittany Mountain takes its name, not to mention Penn State's Nittany Lions football squad) and her lover, who, the legend claims, was drowned in the cave by Nittany's seven overly protective brothers.

Then further west, there is Indian Caverns in Huntingdon County, where a tale is told of Robber Lewis and the cache of gold he hid somewhere near or in that cave (see the chapter titled "Spitzbuben" in the author's *Pennsylvania Fireside Tales Volume IV* for more tales about Robber Lewis and other Pennsylvania highwaymen of that period).

Likewise, to the east in Dauphin County, guides at the cavern known as Indian Echo Cave relate the woeful history of Amos Wilson, also known as the Pennsylvania Hermit. Similarly, at Woodward Cave in Centre County, visitors can hear the legend of Red Panther, a man whose fate was even worse than that of Amos Wilson.

The authenticity of Penn's Cave's legend has been questioned since its source was Henry W. Shoemaker, that well-known embellisher and inventor of similar Central Pennsylvania tales. Shoemaker also published the Red Panther legend, but no one has ever seriously investigated whether or not the story could have a factual basis.

Many students of such things have assumed that Shoemaker may have invented the story since he published it in his romanticized style. However, some clues seem to suggest that the legend, which survived by staying afloat on the currents of oral history, was around long before Shoemaker began writing his entertaining anecdotes.

Anyone wanting to confirm this idea and perhaps hear the version of the story in the way it was probably told to Shoemaker should travel to the small mountain town of Woodward and listen to an aged local resident relate the legend the way they heard it from their parents or their grandparents, who, in turn, had heard it from theirs.

Although that's no longer possible today, as all the old people who knew the original story have passed on to their glory, it was from one such person that I heard the tale one fine day in May some decades ago. The mentally alert seventy-seven-year-old gentleman knew the legends of the place better than anyone, having grown up there and worked there his entire life. His main source was his father, who had helped open the cave for visitors and heard its legends from the old-timers of his day.

"Luther Weaver and Oliver Hosterman opened the cave here in 1926," began the interesting storyteller, "and my dad, Braid, because he was a farmer, was glad for a little extra work. So, during the winter months, he helped clean out the cave. So, I've been around the cave all my life, actually, and my first job was tying on bumper strips. At that time, we didn't paste them on; we tied them on with string.

"And when I was a kid, I heard the cave's legends from my father, including the legend of Red Panther, but over the years, I picked up more on it. Somebody, I believe Lute Weaver, gave me a history of Haines Township, and I read some of that about Red Panther being the son of the chief and about Indians inhabiting the cave.

"Now we knew it as Red Panther's Cave, and that history stated it was close by here in Haines Township. This was the only cave we knew of at the time, and my Dad was saying, 'It must be the cave up here because there's no other cave close by except Penn's Cave.' And it was already open, and they were saying nothing about Red Panther. So, this was the legend about Red Panther as I heard it.

"Red Panther, according to the history, rebelled against the beliefs of the Seneca Indians. They believed that the beech tree was sacred, and there were an awful lot of beech trees around here at one time. There's one right out here yet, and the other one broke down just about three years ago. And that spites me because when I was fourteen years old, I put my name on the side of that beech tree with a pocket knife. Three years ago, that beech broke down, and it split right through where I had my name on, so that's gone. I could've showed you that yet. I put my name on there in the year 1929 and there were a lot of beech trees.

"The same legend says that the Seneca Indians used to gather under beech trees during thunderstorms because they said the beech tree was sacred and lightning would never strike it. In fact, I've never heard of lightning hitting a beech tree either, never. But Red Panther told them he didn't believe in that. He rebelled, and one day, he takes an axe and starts cutting down a beech tree, and while doing so, is struck by lightning and killed. They picked him up, carried him into the cave, and buried him in one of the big rooms. That is the legend of Red Panther. He was the son of the chief."[1]

Some are convinced that the story of Red Panther was indeed invented by a writer like Henry Shoemaker or by owners of the cave as a means of attracting more visitors with a quaint legend. Whatever the case may be, it's still interesting to explore any elements of the tale that may have historical precedents in order to decide whether the legend has any kernels of truth buried in it.

Just fifty years ago, for example, the Amish of Lancaster County would not use lightning rods on houses or barns, preferring instead to have a protective walnut tree growing beside their structures. Their thinking was perhaps similar, although diametrically opposed, to that of the Senecas in the Red Panther legend in that the Amish believed that the walnut tree would somehow attract lightning and divert it away from their house or barn. In both cases, however, the beliefs may have evolved from religious tenets. The Amish ideas, for example, could have risen from early warnings by their bishops.

In the late 1700s and early 1800s, some Scotch-Irish and English ministers, and perhaps clergymen in the various German sects as well, were preaching sermons against the use of lightning rods, seeing them as a means of avoiding the Almighty's justifiable wrath, which to them was irreverent defiance of God himself.[2]

Through a similar thought process, the Delaware Indians of Pennsylvania would not use driftwood to build their sweat lodges because they believed that doing so would cause a flood. They also would not build their lodge houses out of "thunder-burned wood" (wood struck by lightning)

---

1. Ray Stover (born 1912), recorded May 19, 1989.
2. Stevenson W. Fletcher, *Pennsylvania Agriculture and Country Life*, 1640–1840, 504.

Where Red Panther's funeral pyre can be seen. This totem pole at the entrance to Woodward Cave located near Woodward, Centre County, serves as a reminder of the legend of the star-crossed Red Panther whose fate was sealed when he defied the Indian gods and whose funeral pyre can be seen in the cave yet today.

because they were afraid that using such material would anger their lightning spirit. This rage, they thought, would then descend upon them in the form of severe storms.[3]

The fact that both the Amish and the Delaware alike had convictions related to lightning that were slightly similar to the view related in the Red Panther legend lends an air of authenticity to the old tale, thereby making it even more intriguing to those who like to speculate about such connections. But there is more to the story than just the ideas about lightning and beech trees. There is also the question of how the Indians would have handled the burial of a heathen like Red Panther.

History indicates that Indians here in Pennsylvania always treated their dead with utmost respect. The Senecas, for example, would wrap their deceased in skins and place them on scaffoldings, afterward mourning the departed one through a ten-day "death feast."[4] It is also recorded that a dead warrior would never be left on the field of battle, his comrades

---

3. Gladys Tantaquidgeon, *Folk Medicine of the Delaware*, 22.
4. Jesse J. Cornplanter, *Legends of the Longhouse*, 183.

A stark reminder of Pennsylvania's Indian days. This marker, with its inscription "In memory of several Indians, Delaware tribe, buried in this cemetery," can be found in the Salisbury Church graveyard near Allentown, Lehigh County. It is an interesting link to Pennsylvania's frontier history and the Indians who once lived here.

considering it their sacred duty to come back for him so they could drag him away for proper burial.

There may be other pieces of supporting information for the Red Panther legend, and for that matter, for the Penn's Cave legend story, too. Too much time has passed to know for sure in either case, but the old cave guide seemingly had the last word on the authenticity of Woodward Cave's favorite son.

"There's another thing I'm going to mention to you which I never mentioned to anybody. I once did take a family of Seneca Indians through the cave, probably about twenty-two years ago; they had their mother and grandmother with them. So, when we got into the cave, I gave this history about the Seneca Indians.

"They didn't say much about it, but this old lady told me she was one hundred and two years old, and I don't doubt her. Her hair was white as snow, and there was no doubt that she was an Indian. She had her hair in braids, and they hung down almost to her knees in back; and boy, was she witty!

"So, after we showed the cave to them and came back out, this old lady and I sat on a bench outside the entrance. I said to her, 'What do you think about the history we gave you about the Seneca Indians? Do you believe it?'

"'Oh yeah,' she said. 'That's true; they used to live in caves!'

"I said, 'What about Red Panther?'

"'Well, yes,' she said, 'I believe that too because we do believe that the beech tree is sacred, even up to this day!'

"And I said, 'Well, do you think he's buried in there?'

"'Well,' she said, taking a moment to think, 'I don't know. We didn't bury our dead back in those days. Did you ever read about us putting our dead on scaffolds and letting the Great Spirit take care of them?'

"And I looks at her and said, 'Where would he be?'

"She replied, 'Well, your cave has a lot of faults and big cracks in it. Your dead-end room back there has a beautiful one!'

"She walks back under it and looks way up; there's one place in there you can see up about sixty-five feet. And she says, 'There's where they might've buried him—not buried him, but placed him.'

"It made me wonder, and I says to her, 'Well, I'm glad to hear that!'"[5]

Anyone who likes the tales of long ago and wonders about them will probably feel the same way and will appreciate this new perspective on an ancient legend.

5. Ray Stover (born 1912), recorded May 19, 1989.

CHAPTER 2

WOLF DAYS IN CENTRE COUNTY

John Blair Linn, in his timeless *History of Centre and Clinton Counties Pennsylvania,* has preserved a story of a wolf encounter that is probably typical of episodes experienced by early pioneers in many parts of Pennsylvania. This incident from Centre County is said to have occurred in Bald Eagle Township, probably around 1800:

> In the early days, wild animals of various kinds were abundant and, at times, very impudent. On one occasion, as John Carskaddon was on his way to a neighbor's, a distance of a mile or two, he was attacked by a pack of wolves. Their appearance was so sudden, and they assailed him so furiously that he barely had time to take his position against a tree when he killed several of them with his gun, which he happened to have with him before he succeeded in escaping to the house.[1]

It would not be a pleasant experience for anyone to be pursued by a pack of hungry wolves, any one of which is probably strong enough to drag down a man and break his arm or leg with one bite of its vice-like jaws. And even in cases like that of John Carskaddon's, where a person was carrying a musket, being chased by a pack of these terrifying creatures would still be a harrowing ordeal. However, there were times when wolves did pursue early

---

1. John Blair Linn, *History of Centre and Clinton Counties,* 571.

settlers who had no means of defense, and in these instances the experience would have been nothing less than terrifying.

Perhaps that is why several such episodes have managed to survive to the present day through the oral history of Centre County and the following two accounts, both of which have been handed down over the years by the descendants of the individuals who were attacked, reveal unusual strategies that were employed by unarmed men when a gaunt and hungry pack was pursuing them.

The first episode probably occurred in the late 1850s or early 1860s on Big Poe Mountain near the village of Greenbriar, Penn Township, Centre County. Around this time, Solomon Lingle, born in 1836, lived in a log house west of present-day Poe Valley State Park, where he farmed twenty-five or thirty acres of mountain land.

However, his agricultural pursuits fell short of providing all that was needed to support his family, and so Lingle also moonlighted, never missing an opportunity to earn money doing other jobs in order to supplement his meager income. But the story of Solomon Lingle's life and the narrative of his wolf encounter are historical gems saved by his descendants because they preserve a memory of just how tough the people of those times had to be.

"He had a saw mill in Poe Valley and lived in sort of a lean-to there," recalled Lingle's grandson in 1989. "One day, he fell on one of his saws, and it cut open his stomach. He managed to push himself off with his hands, but they were all cut up, too. They put him in a tub of water with his insides all hanging out, but Doc Frank [probably Dr. George S. Frank, who was a physician in Spring Mills and Millheim around 1885] sewed him all up, and he lived a good many years after that!

"Candles were scarce in those days, so at night, his wife, Elizabeth, would hold up a pitch light so he could see to make split wooden shingles to sell. I still have the drawing knife he used to do that. He also would get fifty cents a day, in those days, for mowing other farmers' grass [hay].

"They didn't have reapers then to mow; they would cut it with a scythe. During that harvest time he would start out in the darkness of the early morning hours to make the long walk all the way out of Poe Valley over into Penn's Valley, carrying his scythe on his shoulder.

Home of the old wolf hunter. Still standing at the corner of Penn's Creek Road and the Millheim-Siglerville Pike, it was the home of Jacob Auman, said to have been the killer of the last wolf in the area when he trapped it at the White Sand Spring in the Pine Swamp. The spring can still be seen in the wilds of Big Poe and Long Mountains along the Pine Swamp Road near present-day Poe Valley State Park.

"One morning, when he came down through the Auman Kettle in the Zerby Gap above Greenbriar, he heard a bunch of wolves howling. They wanted to attack him and tried to surround him. He took a stone [the whetstone that was carried by all men who used scythes in those days; the blades of the scythes became dull quickly during the harvest and often had to be resharpened with the whetstones] and hammered it against the blade of the scythe. That scared them and chased them away."[2]

2. Wilbur Wingard (born 1910), interviewed December 24, 1973; recorded November 16, 1989.

Closer view of the old wolf hunter's home. Still standing at the corner of Penn's Creek Road and the Millheim-Siglerville Pike.

Some years earlier, another Centre County man experienced a similar harrowing wolf pack encounter, and his story reveals yet another ingenious way that could be used to ward off a band of these grey marauders. This event took place near Potters Mills, Potter Township, Centre County, sometime during the 1830s or 1840s, and once again, the tale has survived down to the present day because Jonathan Rossman's descendants consider it a unique family heirloom. Born in 1808, Rossman would have been in his early twenties or thirties when he had his brush with death.

"You should probably go back and start with the kind of life Jonathan Rossman had to live," began the family genealogist, who had studied the matter and from whom we were privileged to hear this quaint tale from the olden time.

"He lived in a small cabin in Krise Valley, and here he raised seventeen or eighteen children! My grandfather always told me he was one of seventeen, or he was the seventeenth—I don't recall which it was. Anyway, Jonathan Rossman lived in there, and he raised that family!

"He was what was called a laborer, but maybe I could go a little further and say he was basically a slave. He helped the farmers in Penn's Valley;

families like the Fyes, Fishburns, Mulburgers, and the Wagners. He worked for them all summer and never did anything else.

"Probably, he had a little garden patch, but we don't know for sure because of the way the old foundation has grown over in recent years. But we do know he probably did a lot of hunting, and if I was to guess, I'd say maybe ninety percent of his meat was wild game.

"He also knew a lot about butchering, and in the fall of the year, every day, he would walk, this was his mode of transportation, out Boal Gap Road from Krise Valley and over to Colyer in Penn's Valley to help the farmers butcher. He couldn't go the other way because it was too far to walk to Colyer through the mountains. And this is probably what he did every day of his life in the fall.

"In the olden days, you could hunt anytime, as far as that was concerned, but most of the time, you were done hunting around Thanksgiving because this is when, the fall season, you had things to gather together for the winter. And this is what you always had to do. So, when it got cold enough in the fall, when it come time for butchering, this is the way he spent his time. A lot of his pay was actually in produce—potatoes or cuts of meat from the butchering.

"So, one particular night as he was going home, probably with bloody clothes on because he wouldn't have aprons like butchers have today; he was carrying some sausage and butcher meat. The wolves, attracted by the smells of blood and fresh meat, started chasing him. According to the story, he cleverly fed them the meat and sausage to keep them from attacking him. This tactic allowed him to reach the safety of his cabin, but just as he got inside, the wolves jumped on the porch roof!"[3]

The old gentleman had just handed us one of the best wolf tales we had yet heard in all our years of collecting, but he also left us with a further picture of the people of those times.

"This is the way he fended them off, so he was able to get to his house, and I believe that, without question, this is what happened. But my question to you is, after that, would you be willing to go out tomorrow, leaving before daylight, to make your next appointment? He felt that this was the only way he could maintain his family since butchering came only

---

3. John Wert (born 1912), interviewed July 5, 1981; recorded February 13, 1988.

The Wolf Man's Grave. Said to be the burial place of a werewolf who residents believed was the alpha male of a wolf pack that raided their sheep pens every night along Line Mountain in Northumberland County! See the author's Pennsylvania Fireside Tales *Volume 6 for the strange tale and a possible eplanation behind the mystery.*

once a year. If he missed it, he was missing some food for his family, so he hesitated not one bit!"[4]

There is little reason; it would seem, to doubt that the preceding two wolf encounter accounts happened much like the oral history says they did. At least it seems certain that wolves attacked both men. On the other hand, there may be those who argue that the tales were romanticized by the men in order to impress their friends and families or that some legendary elements got incorporated into the retelling as time passed. In other words, parts of older, similar, episodes could have gotten assimilated into the Lingle and Rossman tales.

It's possible, for example, that accounts of similar wolf attacks that actually occurred in seventeenth- or eighteenth-century Europe were confused with and partially woven into the Centre County folktales. There is,

---

4. Ibid.

in fact, an Irish folktale that contains events that are intriguingly similar to the Lingle and Rossman encounters.

The Irish story referred to has been preserved in a volume of the early history of the British Isles, and it seems worth repeating here, not only because it's such a colorful account but also because it shows that the two tales previously related are, without a doubt, based on fact. The story, with its misspellings, comes from a letter written to Sir James Crofts and dated September 6, 1624:

> A pleasant tale I heard Sir Thomas Fairfax relate of a souldier in Ireland, who having got his passport to go for England, as he past through a wood with his knapsack upon his back, being weary, he sate down under a tree wher he open'd his knapsack and fell to some victuals he had; but upon a sudden, he was surpriz'd with two or three Woolfs, who, coming towards him, he threw some scraps of bread and cheese until all was done; then the Woolfs making a nearer approach unto him, he knew not what shift to make, but by taking a pair of bagpipes which he had, and as soon as he began to play upon them, the Woolfs ran all away as if they'd been scar'd out of their wits. Whereupon the souldier said, "A pox take you all; if I had known you had lov'd musick so well, you should have had it before dinner!"[5]

The similarities between this Irish account and the Centre County ones may mean that there was indeed some partial transfer of details from the one to the others. On the other hand, the similarities more likely indicate that the methods of using food and noise to fend off attacking wolves was not an uncommon tactic used by those who lived in those dangerous yet thrilling times, not just in Centre County but in all parts of Pennsylvania where packs of wolves endangered the lives of people living at a time we now might rightly refer to as Pennsylvania's "wolf days."

NOTE: For those who might have some hesitation in accepting the previous conclusion, the following account, related to Samuel Avery, an early settler of Armenia in Bradford County, may prove of interest. Reuben Nash, who

---

5. James E. Harting, *Extinct British Animals*, 194.

Wolves at the Wolf Sanctuary. The Wolf Sanctuary in Lititz, Lancaster County, Pa., keeps injured and unwanted wolf pets here in nice clean and large pens. The wolves are well cared for and well fed. They are also curious and are used to visitors. As can be seen in the photo, wolves and visitors are securely protected by high double fencing. It still raises the hackles on your neck when they all start to howl as a pack.

lived at nearby Columbia Flats, had asked Avery to help him butcher some hogs, and after working all day, Avery was invited to sit down at the Nash's table for a bountiful supper before trekking back through the four miles of almost unbroken wilderness to his home.

It was dark when the old settler finally headed home carrying a large piece of fresh pork he had received in appreciation for his day's labor. At the last minute, Nash also offered him some "plucks" to take home as well. The plucks, in butchers' parlance, were the pig's heart, liver, and lungs, and the term probably came from the fact that these small delicacies were always plucked from the pig's carcass right after it was slaughtered.

Avery's route took him through a lonely glen called Painter Lick, a name that was not an inviting one considering the denizens of the forest from which its name had been derived and who made it their home from

Several Black Wolves at the Wolf Sanctuary. Curious but still wild, these black wolves kept at the Wolf Sanctuary in Lititz, Lancaster County, Pa., are among several different varieties that can be found here.

time to time. But on this night, it was not panthers Avery had to worry about because he had no sooner entered the dark recess when he heard a pack of wolves howling behind him.

His situation was perilous since he could not return to Nash's to seek safety, and so he made haste for his homestead. But no matter how fast he progressed, the snarling pack kept right up with him and, in fact, seemed to be closing the gap. They finally got so close that Avery could hear their snapping jaws and snarls, and he then resorted to a desperate measure.

Taking his knife, the exhausted pioneer cut off a small piece of the liver "pluck" he had been given and threw it down on the path to the rear. The voracious wolves immediately pounced upon it and fought over it, allowing Avery to put some distance between himself and the predators closing in behind him. He continued sacrificing the liver in this way until he was able to reach the safety of his cabin, thereby saving himself as well as the "bacon" he was also carrying.[6]

6. Reverend David Craft, *History of Bradford County, Pennsylvania*, 264.

NOTE 2: An additional account from the historical annals of Lancaster County also reinforces the idea that those who lived during Pennsylvania's wolf days had to have a lot of courage, or pluck, of their own in order to deal with the threat those gray marauders always posed.

Ludwig Christopher Franciscus, born in 1680, settled in the Conestoga section of Lancaster County in 1710. To his contemporaries, he was known as a "true rough-and-tumble pioneer, large in size and spirit," an opinion that was undoubtedly reinforced by an encounter Franciscus had with a large wolf that invaded his sheep pen one night in 1729.

He had just fallen asleep that night when he was rudely awakened by a chorus of loud and distressing cries coming from his sheep yard. The noise alarmed him so much that he got out of his warm bed and roused his trusty guard dog from its bed as well.

Both dog and master hastened to the fenced-in sheep pen, and just as they got there, a large wolf, alarmed at their approach, tried to escape from the pen by leaping over its fence. In so doing, it got one foot stuck in a small crevice of the fencing, which gave the brave husbandman time enough to act.

Grasping the growling wolf by the neck with his right hand and by one hind leg with the other, Franciscus was able to force the animal to the ground and pin it there by holding its head down with one hand and its body with his knee. It was hard to hold the struggling wolf in this way, especially with the dog biting at it in the rear end, thereby adding to its level of rage.

Finally, the man's calls for help were answered by his oldest daughter Johanna, who, seemingly empowered by genes of courage inherited from her father, came running with a large knife. Once on the scene the fearless girl jumped into the fray and used her knife to disembowel the growling creature her father was wrestling with. It's said that the location where Franciscus' daughter killed the wolf was remembered for years by locals since it was marked by the head of a large spring "near Lampeter Square."[7]

---

7. I. Daniel Rupp, *History of Lancaster County, Pennsylvania*, 85.

CHAPTER 3

LOST TREASURE OF PENN'S CREEK

Few people today are aware of it, but the tale of *Jack and the Beanstalk* preserves an ancient superstition concerning clouds and the treasures people thought they concealed. It was once accepted that clouds were really the mountains of heaven. Apparently solid and impenetrable, these heavenly peaks occasionally seemed to be split apart by jagged bolts of lightning.

During these brief periods of brilliance, it was believed, mere mortals could get a glimpse of the shining wealth within, "but only for a moment, and then, with a crash, the celestial rocks closed again."[1] It was an appealing vision, and fantastic tales were eventually told of lucky souls who had stumbled onto these misty, treasure-laden hills and found their fortunes.

It seems that any stories of lost treasure and yarns about those who have sought it are among the most well-liked of all folktales. Everyone enjoys the idea of discovering a vast fortune that they can keep entirely for themselves. People today try to realize such dreams through participation in the many state lotteries, which anyone can play for a mere dollar or two, but in the old days, peoples' fantasies of getting rich centered around finding buried treasure or stumbling across undiscovered lodes of gold and silver.

Then, too, there evolved a set of beliefs centered around where it was most likely you could uncover such wealth and the exact procedures that

---

1. John Fiske, *Myths and Myth-Makers*, 54.

Jack and the Beanstock. Pencil drawing courtesy Shauna Leva Allen.

had to be followed in order to succeed. So popular and alluring were these notions that they were gradually woven into the folklore of the times, thus creating some of the more interesting tales that once could be found in the quaint corners of Penn's Woods.

In the tale of "Jack's Narrows," for example, which appeared in *The Black Ghost of Scotia and More Pennsylvania Fireside Tales*, the second volume of this series, it was mentioned that people used to believe that great wealth could be found wherever a motionless light would hover over a spot at night. Similarly, it was also once held that certain peculiar formations on the ground were indicative of buried riches.

Any round bare spots in an otherwise fertile field or a circular patch of wet ground where the surrounding soil was dry were believed to be likely places to find buried treasure. This, too, was another tempting idea, and many treasure hunters tried to dig into a *Hexedanz,* believing that the fairies had buried their treasure in these odd barren rings.

However, it was not just a matter of going out any old time and digging away at will; there could be danger facing those who tried and woe to those who didn't do it just right. The hour of the moon had to be exact, and silence had to be maintained throughout the entire time of the excavation. Moreover, popular beliefs held that failure to follow the correct procedures when digging for treasure could result in the loss of the whole thing, as well as possible bodily harm. Nonetheless, that didn't keep men from trying their luck, and there were certainly enough tales of fabulous caches buried here and there in the mountains to keep any avid treasure hunters working full-time.

Almost every county in Pennsylvania has its tale of a gold or silver fortune that was once lost or hidden and now is waiting to be found by some lucky person. In the Sinking Spring Valley of Blair County, for example, there is the story of the canoe-load of gold bullion that two men buried in that region, while Perry County has its own tale of a kettle full of gold that was buried on the site of an Indian burial ground near New Bloomfield.

The Perry County gold was said to have been given to an Indian woman during the French and Indian War by French soldiers in return for English scalps. According to the old tale, the Indians reluctantly left the gold behind when surprised by a vengeful party of attacking settlers who routed them from the area.

Potter County has at least two similar tales, both of lost gold shipments that have never been found; and in McKean County, there is an account of a fortune in silver bars that is buried in the trackless Alleghenies near Smethport. There are a multitude of other similar stories all over the state, but there is one particular Centre County episode that is typical of many of them, and it is included here because it contains a lot of the supernatural elements that were once woven into such narratives.

According to the folktale that has circulated for at least one hundred years along Penn's Creek of Penn's Valley, Centre County, there are two saddlebags filled with gold coins that lay buried in the hills beside the creek. The Indians called this beautiful mountain stream *Kayarondinhagh*, but the settlers decided the Indian title was not worth keeping, and so, inspired by their own self-interests and political agendas, they named it Penn's Creek.

No records seem to have preserved the meaning of the name the Indians assigned to the stream, and, similarly, no one knows today exactly what happened to the gold coins that were once supposedly buried along it, despite the fact that the tale about the coins dates back to a time considerably later than the years when John Penn, son of William Penn, was alive and was honored by having his name placed upon the *Kayarondinhagh* of the Iroquois.

Although the Indians probably had their ancient legends about the stream now called Penn's Creek, the legend of the stream's gold coins is set during the days when soldiers of fortune, con artists, and land speculators were all moving west to try out their get-rich-quick schemes and to see if their luck would be any better in the Ohio Country than the cards fate had dealt them to this point in their lives back East.

Among these adventurers, according to legend, were two horsemen who passed through Central Pennsylvania carrying along their entire fortunes. Their capital consisted of many gold pieces, which the men had stuffed into their saddlebags to be used for land speculation. Undoubtedly, thoughts of the huge profits they would make filled their heads as they traveled through vast tracks of virgin wilderness and into unsettled valleys of unsurpassed beauty. The rest of that story was related to me by a grand old lady who had heard the legend in her youth and who believed it to be true.

"As they rode along," she recalled, "they became aware that they were being followed. So, they rode off the narrow bridle path that ran through the valley and then buried their gold in a thickly overgrown section of forestland where they thought the landmarks could be easily found when they returned to retrieve the coins. They then decided to separate, with the agreement that they would each try to reach the local settlers' fort in the valley called the Upper Fort, or Potter's Fort as it was often referred to in those days, and wait for each other there.

"One of the men actually made it to the old Indian fort, but he had caught a bad cold on the way, and it turned into lung fever. His condition gradually worsened until he realized his companion was most likely never coming and that, unless he confided in someone else, their secret would die with him. As he lay dying, he called a man he had befriended to his bedside and, after swearing him to secrecy, described the location of the hidden gold as nearly as he could."[2]

It was a secret that was not to be kept, and it was from that confidant that the story of the hidden gold became known. The story spread, as treasure stories are apt to do, and from time-to-time people have hunted the gold, but so far as is known, no one has ever found it. Superstition often accompanies such tales, too, and this one is not an exception since some versions say that the place where the gold is hidden is protected by something supernatural.

"More than fifty years ago, my uncle was riding his horse home after a late date one night," continued our storyteller, who claimed to have heard about her relative's weird experience directly from him. "When he came to a deep cut in the road where it was shaded by tall trees and thick brush, he said his horse stopped dead in its tracks."[3]

Maybe it was the darkness, or maybe it was movement on the roadway caused by the moonlit shadows of tree limbs swaying in the night wind, but whatever it was that frightened the animal, the horse suddenly refused to go any further. Its rider tried to force his mount ahead but to no avail until, in one mighty thrust, the horse jumped up onto one of the banks beside the road. Once there it showed no further willingness to move, instead just displaying signs of its fright through violent trembling and rearing up as though about to fight something off.

"At first, he could see nothing," said our elderly storyteller as she continued with the account she had heard from the man who was riding the horse. "But then, when he looked a little longer, he could see an animal about 12 feet long, from the tip of its nose to the tip of its tail. It looked like a panther, but he said it had the feet of a deer, and it also made an unearthly noise unlike anything he had heard before.

---

2. Dorothy Meyer, letter to the author, dated 1978.
3. Ibid.

"At that point, he was too scared to do anything but get out of there the fastest way he knew. He never forgot that spot, nor did his horse, because afterward, every time it came to that same spot, it was always too frightened to pass through, even in broad daylight.

"As time went by and he had a chance to think about it, my uncle said he was convinced that the strange beast he had seen was trying to show where the gold was hidden. Many years later, he revisited the place and actually dug in different spots there, which he thought looked like good places to bury gold. He never found the gold, but he never gave up on the idea that it was there somewhere."[4]

According to our storyteller, the strange events related to her by her Uncle Jerry Corman took place "around 1910 near a farm now owned by the Will Grove family on the Beaverdam Road between Zerby Station and Coburn."[5] Today, the small hill where Jerry Corman dug for the gold still stands behind the barn on the farm once owned by the Bakers. Other people besides Jerry Corman also got the idea that there might be gold hidden on that farm, and it's said that former owners of the place once dug a small hill entirely away in an effort to find the treasure.

Very few people give much thought to the story today, mainly because those who know of the tale have probably concluded that if there ever had been such a treasure, it was probably recovered by the second of the two men who had helped to bury it in the first place and who came back for it at a later date. On the other hand, those who put faith in the old superstitions about how a buried treasure must be excavated might argue that those who dug for this one in the past just didn't know how to do it the right way.

Old folktales have something to say about that, and they preserve several episodes like this that supposedly occurred in various Pennsylvania Dutch sections of the state, including that bastion of the race, the Blue Mountains of Berks and Lebanon Counties.

In their fascinating compilation of Pennsylvania German folk stories collected in the Blue Mountains of the Pennsylvania Dutch country in the early decades of the twentieth century, authors Thomas Brendle and William Troxell mention a number of old anecdotes about quests for buried

---

4. Ibid.
5. Ibid.

wealth, and these same tales preserve the supernatural aura that once was part of the beliefs about treasure hunting.

Based on the Brendle and Troxell tales, it seems that black cats came into play once in a while when people were trying to find a good spot to dig for riches. One suggested method, for example, was to drive a stake into the ground where the fortune was thought to be buried. Then, at night, the treasure hunter was to tie a black cat or a black hen to the stake and come back the next morning. If the fowl or cat was found at that time "torn to pieces, then treasure was there, otherwise not."[6]

The preceding idea begins to touch upon the belief that a buried treasure was oftentimes guarded by something malicious and supernatural, a point also mentioned in the chapter titled "More Snakes," which appears in *Pennsylvania Fireside Tales Volume 2*. In that chapter, it's related that snakes were sometimes thought to be guardians of hidden wealth, but some notions were even more fantastic than this. One such example is a story from Lebanon County, which is said to have occurred shortly after the Revolutionary War.

During this time of upheaval and new beginnings there was a bandit who was the terror of southern Lebanon County, or so the story goes. He was very successful in plying his cowardly trade, and since he couldn't take his ill-gotten gains to a bank for safekeeping, the notorious thief elected instead to bury his loot at well-concealed and inaccessible spots in the South Mountains. The work of concealing the plunder would always be done at night so no one would notice, but this made it hard for the criminal to find the places where he wanted to retrieve some of his stash.

In order to overcome this problem, the clever thief tied a string to a tree along the mountain pass and stretched it over to the spot where his loot was buried. This marked the hiding place to his satisfaction and enabled him to find it at night, until one day when the string somehow got broken. After that time, the treasure was lost, and the thief himself could never find it again.

Eventually, the robber died, but the stories of his buried caches lingered on and were convincing enough that a group of local men decided to try their luck at finding it. Before doing so, however, they decided that they

6. Thomas R. Brendle and William S. Troxell, "Pennsylvania German Folk Tales, Legends, Once-upon-a-time Stories, Maxims, and Sayings," *Proceedings of the Pennsylvania German Society, Volume L*, 58.

first needed to consult a well-known seeress who, they had heard, owned a magical mirror that would help lead them to the spot they were seeking.

They went to see the local woman, and she advised them to go to a particular spot in the area and draw some sort of magical circle on the ground. They were then to dig only within the circle, taking care not to throw any dirt outside of it when they were digging for the treasure.

The men drew the circle according to the directions given to them, and then they excitedly began to dig. After a lot of hard labor, they had managed to dig a shoulder-deep hole, and then one of the diggers discovered a chest. Just as he was about to cry out that he had found it, he looked up and saw a "large black dog with jaws open and teeth bared, ready to leap on him."[7]

The sight of the ferocious dog frightened him so much that he instinctively reacted by striking at the beast with his shovel. But when he did so a little dirt that was still on the shovel landed outside the circle, and "immediately the dog vanished, and also the chest."[8]

Similar tales of the Blue Mountains told of men finding treasure chests but of being thwarted by the sudden appearance of a "ferocious looking boar,"[9] or by a dragon, or by the devil himself. It's said that treasure hunters over in Findland, Montgomery County, for example, once searched for a buried fortune in that part of the state; and had also been told that silence had to be maintained "from the time they began to dig until they had the treasure fully in their possession."[10] The treasure hunters dug away, never saying a word until they found the chest.

Excited by their good fortune, the men grabbed the handles of the chest and hoisted it above their heads. They had lifted the chest about half way to the surface when one man looked up. He was so surprised and frightened by what he saw that he forgot the code of silence and yelled, "Drop it! The man with the red jacket!" [*Der mit em rode wammes*—another name used for the devil]. Immediately," according to the legend, "the chest disappeared."[11]

---

7. Ibid, 48.
8. Ibid, 48.
9. Ibid., 46.
10. Ibid., 49.
11. Ibid., 53.

This last example from the Blue Mountains shows just how intense the superstition surrounding treasure hunting could be, and, along with the other stories like it, provides clues as to where people might have gotten the idea that a frightful beast once guarded treasures like the one that was said to be buried along Penn's creek.

All kinds of frightful imaginings could occur in the mind of a person who had heard such tales from the time they were young and who suddenly was thrown into a set of circumstances that seemed to bring all the old beliefs to life. All it would take would be the night wind wailing through the trees, causing dried leaves and dead branches to rattle like the bones of some forgotten skeleton.

Add these macabre effects to some dark clouds flitting across a cloud-shrouded moon that was casting shadows of swaying tree limbs on the road ahead, and the setting would be just right for anyone's imagination to run wild. In Jerry Corman's case, there was the additional stimulus of his passing through the dark ravine where a treasure was supposedly once hidden.

Perhaps just at that same time, a large bobcat or even a mountain lion crossed the road in front of him. That certainly would have been enough to startle the horse he was riding and, if the cat was big enough, enough to cause his mind to work overtime. When that happened, he may have started to see things that weren't really there at all, including subconscious images formed in his mind by tales he had once heard as a boy.

As far as the treasure itself, on the other hand, maybe it's still there. If so, then perhaps another Jack, like the young boy in the fairy tale, will be walking through the woods along Penn's Creek one day and will be distracted by a golden flash of light as the sun is reflected off something partially exposed in a hill along the creek. The boy may rush to investigate and at that point, find the long-lost treasure at last. If so, he will be hailed as a modern-day version of the Jack of fairy tale fame, except he will have had to fight neither giants nor monsters in order to carry away his fortune.

CHAPTER 4

THE TELLTALE TOMBSTONE

I nnocent until proven guilty is one of the basic cornerstones of our legal system, but this seems only to hold for the living. Sometimes, the dead can be unjustly accused of crimes and, with no way to defend themselves, are, in these cases, tried and convicted in the minds of the living without so much as a trial or benefit of a lawyer. Unfortunately, there probably have been many situations like this throughout history, but there is one long-lived Centre County instance in particular which, when brought to their attention, can still enrage descendants of the defamed.

This story is not recalled or frequently retold anymore, but it does still surface now and then, particularly on All Hallows Eve when ghost stories are passed around fireplaces and camp fires. However, this was not the case 90 or 100 years ago when the yarn was well-known by residents of the many small settlements surrounding the tiny Centre County village of Millheim.

The episode was probably a favorite topic of conversation at auctions, flittings, camp meetings, and other social events of the day. And certainly, it would have been a hot item that was often heard around the pot-bellied stoves of country stores in adjacent communities like Aaronsburg, Rebersburg, Madisonburg, Spring Mills, Wolfe's Store, and Farmers Mills at the turn of the twentieth century.

Numerous theories could be proposed to account for the tale's popularity, but the primary reason that explains why it was destined to be more than just a seven-day wonder is that it's the type of account that is designed to activate even the most lackluster imagination. After all, when you have a murder mystery woven into the plot and supernatural evidence that seems to lead to the murderer, it's hard for most people not to be intrigued and to wonder if, indeed, such things can actually happen.

No less than seven versions of the Millheim legend have surfaced over the years, but whether the murderer's victim is a child, another man, or a woman, the instrument of death is always a knife, for if it were something else there would be no telltale tombstone. However, there does exist just such a gravestone, and it sits in a prominent position within the hallowed ground of the town's Union Cemetery—a quaint country burial plot that lies just west of the town whose name, when translated from the German, means "Home of the Mills."

The location of the telltale tombstone seems appropriate since Millheim was also known at one time for its-bleak-looking haunted house, which still sits on a high knoll on the left side of the road as you enter town from the west. The building was left unoccupied for a long time, being mainly used for storage, and signs of neglect became more and more noticeable as the years went by until, finally, the place began to take on a look that was more in line with its reputation. However, in 1997, the rundown house was finally repaired or spruced up, as they might say, in that part of the country.

How that upgrade has affected its ghostly resident seems unclear, for like most neglected places, this house has, or has had, its ghost as well, and its story may be included in a future *Fireside Tales* volume. It's a tale that is just perfect for a book like this, not unlike that of the tombstone in the Union Cemetery, which, although standing almost unnoticed and forgotten these days, preserves the memory of the man who became the target of the vicious rumors that surfaced some years after his death.

It seems that Daniel A. Musser was a success story of no small proportions relative to many of his contemporaries. Born in 1822 into one of the oldest pioneer families of the state, Musser grew up as a farm boy in the Gregg Township area of Centre County, but when he turned eighteen, he learned the ways of the miller's trade.

The young man had no education beyond that which he had gotten at the country school houses of the day, but he was a fast learner who had inherited some of his father's keen business sense. For two years, he successfully managed his father's grist and saw mills, but eventually, the pleasant song of the mill wheel lost its charm, and the splashing waters of Elk and Penn's Creeks beckoned him on to new adventures and higher accomplishments.

Today, a person like Daniel Musser would, no doubt, be called a Type A personality; that is, someone who is always active and who seems to be involved in many different things at once. Based on his track record, Musser was not one to let any grass grow under his feet. After leaving the family businesses, he went on to establish an impressive list of accomplishments of his own, including being elected Deputy Sheriff of Centre County and then County Treasurer.

He also found the time to be an avid hunter, holder of many township offices, a leader in his church and Sunday school, a beloved father who raised a family of seven children, and an owner of lucrative lumber, tanning, foundry, and flour mill businesses. That he was a very successful man is clearly evident from the fact that at the time of his death in 1888, he owned two large flour mills, as many farms, and other parcels of real estate around Millheim.

Based on such an impressive record of lifetime service and accomplishments, Daniel Musser would seem to be one of those individuals who, in his day, would have been popularly described as one of nature's noblemen. However, despite all the evidence to the contrary, Musser was to become known as the perpetrator of a foul crime—one which may not have ever even been committed at all. Nonetheless, once the story of the deed surfaced, it became popular fodder for the gossip mills and slander carriers of the town, so that to this day, the old legend still besmirches the man's name and robs his descendants of the pride that should be rightfully theirs.

Contrary to what one might normally expect, the rumors about Daniel Musser and the crime he supposedly committed surfaced only after the man had been dead and buried for about 30 or 40 years. And it all started because of the appearance of an unusual image on his tombstone.

Shaped from a fine block of granite or some other type of rock that would outlast less durable material, Musser's marker stands much taller than those around it. This noticeable difference in height is enough by itself to draw peoples' attention to it, and the fact that it sits close to the main road into town was also, it turns out, another unexpected disadvantage.

Musser's family probably thought that such an esteemed member of the community should be buried in a prominent spot in the local cemetery, but they could not have foreseen that a less visible plot might have been better. How could they have known that nature, in one of her cruel twists of fate, would place a brand on the memorial—a mark which would be as insinuative as that of the scarlet A, which the heroine was forced to wear in Nathaniel Hawthorne's famous novel entitled *The Scarlet Letter*?

In Hawthorne's fictional work, Hester Prynne is forced to pin a large scarlet letter A on the chest area of her dress in order to prominently display it at all times as punishment for having committed adultery. It would be a cruel and unusual punishment, to say the least, always having to display a sign that would let everyone who met you know that you were a sinful outcast, but Daniel Musser's reputation was just as sullied by the mark that was indelibly stamped upon him as well—or, to be more exact, upon his tombstone.

For the outlines of the knife that mysteriously appeared on it, decades after the headstone was put into place, and which some said actually dripped blood at times, was no less damning than Hester Prynne's scarlet letter. The only difference, it might be said, was that Hester was depicted as being alive when she had to bear the abuse of her accusers, whereas Daniel was mercifully spared such shame; instead, it was his descendants who suffered the injustice of it all.

Perhaps there was a murder, or murders, in the Millheim area during Daniel Musser's lifetime, and local historians may be able to verify the truth of the matter. However, if there were any crimes like that at all during this period, it would take a lot of reading through editions of old newspapers to find any details today. No doubt, Aaronsburg's *Der Centre Berichter*, published from 1827 through 1871 before it was moved to Millheim to become the *Millheim Journal*, would have published articles on any crime as sensational as murder.

But stories recorded on the ephemeral pages of newspapers are not destined to be long-lived, and so a lot of things that were of great importance to the people of that day are no longer even remembered today—even crimes of great passion. Certainly, the late Donald Heggenstaller, colorful entrepreneur and last editor of the *Millheim Journal*, would have been as likely as anyone to know some of the details about past murders in the area, but he knew of none other than the infamous case of William Ettlinger— an Old West type of shootout which occurred in nearby Woodward in 1896, and which will be the subject of a story in a future volume of my *Pennsylvania Fireside Tales* series.

Heggenstaller, an interested and discerning observer of his fellow country folk and a dabbler in things unusual and fantastic had heard several versions of the Musser tale. One of those accounts claimed that a murder supposedly once occurred in the Millheim Hotel and that Daniel Musser was suspected as the murderer. However, the version that Haggenstaller printed in his *Millheim Journal* was the one that invoked the wrath of several of Musser's descendants.

In 1988, Heggenstaller recalled that story for me once again: a legend that states that Musser came home one day and found that his new bride had been brutally murdered with a butcher knife. This rendition goes on to state that despite his claims of innocence and evidence supporting that claim, local people still refused to believe the young bridegroom was not the killer, and so Musser was eventually tried, found guilty, and hanged for the crime.

In what the tale seems to see as Musser's final desperate attempt to convince his accusers of his innocence, the tormented man is said to have uttered last words something to the effect that "If I'm innocent you shall know, a knife from my gravestone shall grow!"[1]

"Oh my God!" recalled Heggenstaller. "My phone rang from those family members. 'How could I disgrace their name?' Oh, did we have a dandy over that deal! But what the tombstone story actually does is to clear him of this murder he was supposed to have been blamed for. He had made comment that there would be a knife, and I was told by people like old Bob Colyer here in Millheim, he's been dead for twenty-eight years, that it actually happened; that a knife came out on that tombstone and that it actually dripped blood!

---

1. Becki Brown, "Ballad of Millheim Cemetery," October 26, 1972 article in *The Millheim Journal* (Donald Heggenstaller, editor).

The Telltale Tombstone. In the Union Cemetery, just outside Millheim, Pa.

"So they turned the tombstone around," continued Heggenstaller, "and the knife came out on this side again. They finally plastered it over, and that didn't do it. Now, there's a metal plate on both sides. The family says the metal plates were put there because the tombstone cracked, and they're trying to keep it together!"[2]

Although the tombstone is real (it stands there in the same spot in the cemetery where it was originally erected), as are the metal plates upon it, the idea that Daniel Musser was hanged for his supposed crime is pure fiction since it's well documented that he died of natural causes. However, the notion that he was responsible for someone else's death seemed to take on a life of its own over the years.

One variation of the tombstone legend states that he murdered a child with a butcher knife, and the image of that same knife was placed on Musser's gravestone, presumably by supernatural forces of some sort, to identify him as the murderer.

Still, another rendition of the tale relates that he betrayed a young maiden and then, apparently to keep her from tarnishing his reputation, killed her. It was her vengeful spirit—the last remaining essences of this

2. Donald Heggenstaller (born 1936), recorded November 18, 1988.

rejected mountain maid whose life, so full of promise, was taken away in such a violent fashion—that caused the knife to appear on the tombstone as evidence of Musser's guilt, or at least that's what this particular version of the legend claims. But there is yet another spin on the story, and it also clings to the theme of the scorned young maiden.

"This here young girl, she might have been fourteen or fifteen and was maybe an orphan or something like that," recalled yet another popular teller of valley tales, "had been housekeeping for this Musser family. She became pregnant, and then she got murdered somehow. They first said her death was an accident, but then they accused this man Musser of doing it.

"They never convicted him because, you know, people around here; they go by your status. They don't give a damn what you do as long as you go to church every Sunday and have lots of money—that's all that matters! So that was his position, too. Of course, some of the lesser people accused him; the common people talked. But he said if he had killed her, there would be a knife on his tombstone!"[3]

Injurious as these tales are, it would seem that to some people, the smears were not black enough. Although the rumors pointed to Musser as a cold-blooded murderer, some apparently were not satisfied with what the stories claimed was the motive behind his crime. A slaying of a young and helpless woman always made for a good plot in a mystery novel, but there had to be money involved in a real murder story, and Musser obviously wasn't lacking funds; at least, that would seem to be a possible explanation as to why one other version of the legend surfaced. Whether or not it became more popular than all the others is hard to say, but it definitely added a new twist to the story line.

According to this rendition, the murder committed by Daniel Musser occurred during the tumultuous war years of 1861–1865. The War Between the States certainly was a time, it would seem, that caused everyone's nerves to be a bit more on edge, and so it might occur to someone who wanted to come up with a good story that if a murder were going to be committed, it might be during the Civil War.

Despite the anxieties and stresses of that period in Pennsylvania history, the husbandman had to continue his day-to-day tasks, and so the business,

---

3. Jean Voneida (born 1934), recorded November 13, 1982.

some in those days, would say the backbreaking drudgery of farming continued as usual. There were still fields to plow, crops to plant, and cattle to raise; and during those times, it was a common sight during the late spring and summer months, to see herds of cattle or packs of horses being driven to market by men called drovers. It was one such drover that figures in the Civil War version of the Daniel Musser tombstone story.

In order to set the stage for this account from the Civil War years, a few words should first be said about drovers in general. The period from 1810 to 1840 has been described as "the golden age of the drover."[4] Droves of sheep, swine, horses, cattle, and even flocks of turkeys were common sights in certain sections of Pennsylvania during that period, and the passing of three or four such droves through the same area in a single day was not uncommon.

There was certainly enough economic incentive to warrant such drives, since local farmers would buy some of the moving stock as the drover guided his animals over high mountains and into valleys of the back country. There was also an incentive because of seasonal advantages. Back roads were almost impassable to wagon traffic during the spring thaws, but could still be traversed by four-legged travelers no matter how deep the mud. It was, therefore, likely that whenever going to or coming back from the market, the drover might be carrying cash, a fact that evidently didn't escape the inventor of the Musser legend that is set during the Civil War.

After over 100 years, there is not much left except the bare bones of the story, but the report was probably always sketchy. After all, it's pretty hard to come up with details sometimes when there is no honest basis for the tale in the first place. Nonetheless, the legend from the 1860s states that in those days, drovers would bring horses and cows through Penn's Valley, selling and buying as they went along.

The drovers, as noted earlier, carried the money they made along with them, and one morning, one of these itinerant cowboys was found in a ramshackle barn just outside of Millheim. The man had been stabbed to death, and his stash of cash was not on his body. It was from this ill-gotten gain, the tale claims, that Daniel Musser got his start, for it was Musser, continues the legend, who robbed the unfortunate drover after killing him with a knife.[5]

---

4. Stevenson W. Fletcher, *Pennsylvania Agriculture and Country Life*, 1640–1840, 179.
5. Dorothy Meyer (born 1915), interviewed November 24, 1972.

The account of the murdered drover was probably as earnestly told and as fervently believed as all the other versions of the same legend. However, at some time or another, each variation of the tale was no doubt touted as the one true story behind the damning evidence, evidence in the form of a strange image that actually did appear on Daniel Musser's tombstone. And there is no doubt that a stain or flaw, roughly in the shape of a knife, did eventually become visible on the Musser grave marker.

Many people saw the likeness, and most agreed that it certainly looked like a knife blade. What was even more wondrous, however, was where the instrument of death appeared, on a sacred place like a tombstone. There had to be something supernatural about the whole thing, and through the 1920s, spectators were still lining up to get a look at the marvelous picture. The more people looked at it, the more bizarre it seemed, and soon, stories surfaced that claimed the dagger would actually drip blood at certain times, particularly when it rained.

Local children, especially those living near the cemetery, were often too scared to go out at night because of the tales, but they mortified Daniel Musser's descendants, who finally took steps to eliminate the ugly scar on the stone. Local accounts say the family tried a number of different approaches, including using acid to dissolve the image, turning the stone around, replacing the whole marker twice, and so on.

But in all cases, the image came back until a metal plate was finally placed over it, and that seems to have done the trick. Nonetheless, there are those yet today who claim that on rainy days, a strange substance oozes out from under the metal plate, a substance that looks like blood.

To those who look for logical explanations for such things, and this writer is among them, let it be said that flaws do occasionally appear on rocks, and they often do bear a close resemblance to a real object. Moreover, when this happens on a tombstone, and it sometimes does, all sorts of weird and sometimes malicious tales surface about the person the stone memorializes. In fact, there are at least two such instances that should be mentioned, either one of which can provide some measure of comfort to the long-suffering descendants of Daniel Musser.

The first prominent case of these telltale tombstone stories involves a marker in the cemetery at Bucksport, Maine, where a gravestone over the burial place of Colonel Jonathan Buck has fascinated the curious for almost one hundred and fifty years. Jonathan Buck was the founder of the little New England town that still bears his name, and, like many of his contemporaries, the colonel was a strict believer in the old Puritanical beliefs, including the idea that a witch should not be allowed to live.

One day, so the story goes, it was brought to the Colonel's attention that one elderly woman of the town was accused of being a witch; and feeling the evidence was damning enough, the autocratic town father ordered her to be burned at the stake. The unfortunate victim expired in the flames, which burned off one of her legs completely.

But before she died, say the old accounts, she screamed a curse at the Colonel, saying that upon his tombstone would appear a sign that would mark him as the murderer of an innocent woman. At first, it seemed to be an empty threat because after Buck died in 1795, his marker of gray Maine granite stood unblemished for fifty-seven years. But then, in 1852, people began to notice an unusual outline on the stone, a form that looked like the small foot and leg of a woman.

Although the Jonathan Buck legend begins to show that there are indeed other tombstone flaws that have led to fantastic stories, the Maine image is not that of a knife. However, the second prominent legend involving a telltale tombstone falls closer to home; and this story does involve many facets that closely resemble the Millheim legend, including the picture of a knife on the gravestone.

This other Pennsylvania telltale tombstone sits in a small country graveyard in Sullivan County, and it's not an altogether unfitting place for it to be since morbid curiosities like it needs to be surrounded by something uplifting and beautiful—a place like Sullivan County. Justly called Pennsylvania's Highlands, Sullivan County is home to wonderful natural wonders like the majestic World's End State Park and beautiful Eagles Mere Lake, but it also has its share of legends, including the Sullivan County man who was condemned to die in the electric chair for killing another man with a knife.

The Sullivan County murderer claimed he was innocent and loudly proclaimed that he hoped the Almighty would mark his tombstone somehow to show the truth. His protestations were to no avail, and after he was executed, his family erected a nice marker over his resting place.

The dead man's wish for a mark on his tombstone did not take long to be fulfilled, for shortly after his internment, an outline that looked like a knife slowly began to materialize on the surface of the granite. Then, as time wore on, the image took on more definite detail, and people could clearly see something under the dagger: spots that looked like drops of blood that had dripped off the blade.

Immediately, people concluded that the Almighty had answered the man's prayers, but not as he had expected; He had put the telltale image on his tombstone to show that he was guilty as charged and had not been unjustly put to death after all. Such talk disturbed the man's family, and so they chiseled the image off the marker. However, the indelible mark came back in short order, and so they replaced the stone altogether. That, too, did not keep the unholy stain from coming back, and "the same thing happened again—the dagger and the blood."[6]

Since it's now obvious that several bloody accounts similar to the Musser tombstone legend have surfaced in other areas over the years, it is left to readers to decide whether or not the legend of Millheim's telltale tombstone preserves underlying evidence that points to Daniel Musser as a murderer. However, the fact that strikingly similar tales and circumstances have appeared in other places is reason enough to have little faith in any historical truths claimed by the Millheim legend.

Moreover, given the history of the man and noting his many positive accomplishments, it seems more than safe to say that he has been wrongfully accused these many decades. Perhaps there was a Millheim murderer who committed a crime there that was as dastardly as one described in one of the versions of the Musser legend, but it's unlikely that the culprit was the man who a biographer of the times once described as one whose "home and family stood first in his affections, and throughout his wedded life the dearest place on earth was his own fireside."[7]

6. James York Glimm, *Flatlanders and Ridgerunners*, 123.
7. J. H. Beers and Company, *Commemorative Biographical Record of Central Pennsylvania*, 337.

CHAPTER 5

TAKING FIRE FROM A GUN

As my years of collecting went by and I accumulated more and more legends and folktales from many different parts of Pennsylvania, I began to see that quite a few of the same stories that had circulated during the 1800s were still alive and well during the 1900s.

Stories of fantastic animals, fabulous treasures, lonely ghosts, and mysterious witches had not disappeared altogether, but they were fading fast. In fact, today, you would not be able to hear many of the types of tales that I could still find when I started looking for them in 1970, and this is especially true of the witch tales. Among the strangest types of stories a collector could find in those days, the old-time witch stories provide us with some entertaining reading and a reminder of something we all should take seriously right now.

I would expect that many readers of these old-style witch tales will sooner or later begin to think that the people who lived on the farms, in the wooded valleys, and on the rugged mountain slopes of rural Pennsylvania at the start of the twentieth century had a special feeling about their time and place; a feeling that there was something marvelous and mystical about these grand hills after all.

Certainly, some of these feelings were due to the superstitions that were entrenched in the culture of the mountains, but there was more to it than that. And I think the answers can be found today just by looking out over the vistas offered from some of our mountain peaks or by taking a hike through the grandest parts of our forests.

A Clinton County hunter's mountainside tent camp of the 1920s. Taken along the east branch of Big Run, Sproul State Forest. Photo courtesy Pennsylvania State Archives, Public Relations Office, Photo file #176, RG-6, Dept. of Forest and Waters.

However, we need to remember that this is a vulnerable environment and then take the steps necessary to preserve it for all time. If we don't it will disappear, leaving future generations with the feeling that we didn't understand the mechanisms of nature any better than those who once believed in witches.

One of the things that surprised me the most in talking to old-timers about their witch tales was that, at one time people believed in supernatural explanations for natural phenomena that most of us fully understand today. I've heard some very strange accounts like this over the years, a few of which have appeared in the first two volumes of this series, and among the strangest were the tales about the game that could not be shot due to the fact that a witch had placed a spell upon it or a hunter's gun.

This was once a very common type of story that could be heard wherever Pennsylvania hunters gathered to talk of the chase, and they even had explanations as to how it was all done. In fact, one of their ideas was that a witch could, in the Pennsylvania Dutchman's language, *es feier nemme*, or "take the fire from the gun."[1]

At one time in Pennsylvania Dutch land, many believed that such a thing was possible, that a witch or powwower could invoke a charm that would render someone's gun harmless. It was thought that this effect was accomplished either by preventing the powder from igniting or by causing the shot to dribble harmlessly out the end of the gun barrel after the powder discharged. Undoubtedly, beliefs like this were more prevalent in the days when a man's rifle was most likely a muzzleloader—the kind that Davy Crockett or Daniel Boone once carried.

Notoriously slow to load, the so-called Kentucky rifle was originally crafted by Swiss and German gunsmiths in Pennsylvania for use on the unsettled Pennsylvania frontier of the 1700s. Improvements were made to them as decades went by, but the guns still were often prone to misfire if their priming hole was clogged or if their powder was damp, and the expression "flash in the pan" comes from the flintlock rifle days when a man pulled the trigger to fire his gun and the only thing that happened was the flash and the smoke of the powder in the rifle's firing "pan," which was the flat outer surface directly above the priming hole.[2]

Just enough gunpowder was placed on the pan to ignite the powder in the hole, which in turn would ignite the powder in the rifle barrel. It took a steady aim to hit anything with a flintlock due to the delay between the time the trigger was pulled and the instant the gun actually discharged. Needless to say, if a man pulled the trigger and made a concentrated effort to remain absolutely steady until the gun discharged, he would be a little upset if nothing happened. However, his patience would be even more severely tried if his gun's misfiring meant a particularly nice buck would fall to another hunter's bullet or that he didn't get that grouse or rabbit for his family's next meal.

Unshootable grouse seem to be a favorite game animal when it comes to tales of witches taking fire from guns, and such stories have been around a long time. Berks County had its share of these kinds of yarns,

1. Thomas R. Brendle and William S. Troxell, "Pennsylvania German Folk Tales, Legends, Once-upon-a-time Stories, Maxims, and Sayings," *Proceedings of the Pennsylvania German Society, Volume L*, 58.

2. Samuel E. Dyke, *The Pennsylvania Rifle*, 13.

A Pennsylvania Long Rifle. Typical of the flintlocks once used by early Pennsylvania frontiersmen and hunters, they were not entirely reliable as far as firing when the trigger was pulled and the powder was damp.

and undoubtedly most other Pennsylvania Dutch sections of Pennsylvania did as well. One typical tale of this type from central Centre County, for example, recalls an episode that involves Benny Ripka of Spring Mills, one of that area's best-known powwowers.

Ripka was famous over a wide area for the miracles he could perform in counteracting the spells of bad witches. He was often called upon to cure sick cattle, to quiet crying children, or to help anyone in general who thought they had been bewitched in one way or another. There were many stories about the sly conjurer's feats that made the rounds over the years, and at least one of them concerned the time that he was accused of taking fire from a gun.

Ben Ripka was never known for his hunting exploits, but he did have a collection of old muzzle-loading rifles at his homestead in the gap that was named after his family. Here in Ripka Gap, an isolated cut through the wilds of Big Poe and Sand mountains, Ripka tended an apple orchard on land that had belonged to his family since the early 1800s. He farmed some of that acreage, but in the back of his house, on soil that was not suitable for farming, he grew apple trees. His stand of trees produced plenty of fruit every year, enough that he could use it to make cider to sell to others.

That he was somewhat successful in his efforts is evidenced by the fact that he eventually made his wooden barrels in which to sell his apple squeezings, and he may have even had a large steam-driven press, like those so popular at that time, to dice and squeeze the apples fed into it.

If so, it may have been one much like Harry Neff's old press that has been preserved and is still used every fall at the mountain estate known as the *Bergheim* in Decker Valley of Centre County. For those who are intrigued by unusual names and their origins, I should mention here that Cider Press Road, along Route 322 and near the village of Potters Mills, was named after Neff's press, which once stood along this country byway, and which I helped to load onto a flat-bed wagon and move from there to the *Bergheim*!

However, what does seem certain after all this time is that for many years, when the invigorating spell of autumn spilled over the land, turning leaves to gold, tinting skies with the purest of blue, and cloaking awakening valleys with a blanket of morning white, Ben Ripka could be found cider pressing or making cider barrels. His hard work kept him fit, or so it would seem since one of his contemporaries remembered him as being a "fairly tall and thin" man and "never too dressed up."[3]

Jared Ripka, an old-time lumberman from Spring Mills, during an interview in 1971, also recalled that his powwowing relative was a bit of a prankster, who "liked to put something over on others."[4] After recalling this interesting trait, Mr. Ripka was also reminded of one particular incident where Bennie's sense of humor led to some hard feelings: the time when old man Billy Walburn thought he was going to have a nice roasted grouse for supper but got mad instead.

It seems that Billy Walburn showed up at Ben Ripka's barrel shop one day after noticing three grouse perched in a couple of Bennie's apple trees out back. He asked him if he could borrow one of his muzzleloaders to shoot the birds. After studying the situation for a moment, Ripka took down one of his flintlocks and handed it to Walburn with the comment, "Take this one; it's loaded, too." Walburn immediately went out back, took aim, and fired at the birds in the apple trees.

At first, it must have seemed to the rifleman that the birds were deaf because even though he had gotten fairly close when the gun went off, the birds didn't fly away. Then, probably as he thought about it more and more and finally was unable to convince himself there was a natural explanation for the bird's seeming indifference to his assault, Walburn began to think

---

3. Jared B. Ripka (born 1885), interviewed August 27, 1971 and February 2, 1974.
4. Ibid.

of other explanations, finally settling on the idea that Ripka had taken the fire from the gun.

The cider maker categorically denied the charge and handed his accuser another muzzleloader, saying, "Here, take this one." This was too much of an insult for the old man, and he "stormed off in a huff." But just as Walburn was stomping away, Ripka took the second gun and went out back. Taking careful aim, he shot two of the grouse with a single shot.

After picking up the dead birds, the marksman then stated that he would "just take these over and give 'em to Walburns." However, that was to be a harder task than it seemed, for when the grouse were offered to the Walburns, the old man refused them, even though his family was poor. He was still "fallen out" with the man who he presumed had taken the fire from his gun.[5]

Other similar accounts like this could be heard in these same mountains, and it seems each one has a unique flavor. Take this next example, where a woman was suspected of taking the fire from several hunters' guns. The setting for this tale is in an area of Centre County referred to locally as The Loop because it's noted for the confusing way the many country roads through here wind around in a manner that can bewilder the unsuspecting traveler.

"When they went up through [the Loop] with their shotguns," recalled the son of one of the frustrated hunters mentioned in the story, "some old woman said, 'Where're you goin'?' And they said, 'For grouse!' She said, 'Aw, you ain't gonna get anything today anyway!'

"They went up there, and they shot, and they shot, and they shot. Nothing! They saw lots of them, and they couldn't hit 'em! Then, when they came back down through, the old woman met them at the yard gate where they had first seen her. This time, she was holding her apron up, and she says, 'Here, boys, I'll give you your shot back!' And Daddy said her apron was full of it. He said, 'I seen that with my own eyes!'"[6]

Although witches' spells were once believed to have saved quite a few grouse from the deadly fire of a hunter's gun, rabbits, too, were thought to

---

5. Jared B. Ripka (born 1885), interviewed August 27, 1971 and February 2, 1974.
6. Harry Brown Jr. (born 1926), recorded May 21, 1989.

be sometimes protected in the same way, and the following examples are typical of those tales.

"The mountains was full of witchcraft," claimed the lifelong country girl who was born in 1904. "The Confers, the Aumans, and the Oxenreiders lived in there in Poe Valley, and them Confers and Aumans was noted for that!"

"I was in there, right there in Voneida Gap where you go up through to the left," chimed in her husband, picking up on his wife's witchcraft theme, "and there was a lot of weeds in there. So, thinks I, I'll just drive over there, and I'll shoot a couple of rabbits. I took the twelve gauge shotgun and went over. There was lots of rabbits, but I couldn't hit 'em! They just hopped away! Well, I blamed Ralph L. and his wife. They live right below here, and I blamed them since they seen me go up and they heard me shoot. They were into that kind of [witchcraft] business. And you know, after that, I couldn't hit nothin' with that gun!"[7]

One other long-time resident of the same area had a similar problem one day when he was out hunting for rabbits. Schoolteacher Clarence Musser was not a superstitious person, and so he was not easily swayed by talk of enchanted game or of witches who would take the fire from a man's gun. Although he was born in 1884 when superstition still ruled a lot of peoples' lives, Musser had acquired enough education to know a little bit about the natural laws of the universe. He knew that the old wives' tales about witches and their seemingly supernatural powers were just poor attempts to explain away events that, in all probability, had logical explanations if enough thought and time were devoted to an investigation.

Armed with this kind of rational thinking, Musser did not hesitate a minute one day in 1907 when he decided to hunt rabbits up on the Brown farm near the quaint burial ground known as the mountain cemetery. The would-be rabbit hunter knew that a man named "Hen" Zerby, who had a reputation as a powerful witch, lived in this area and that Zerby's greatest fame came from his power to bewitch animals so no hunters could shoot them. The general opinion was that the mountain wizard had the whole area around him enchanted so that no one who hunted there could shoot a deer, a grouse, a rabbit, or any other kind of game.

---

7. Randall Steiger (born 1904), and wife, recorded May 4, 1988.

"I said I'd get rabbits," recalled the old schoolteacher in 1971. "I was teaching at the mountain schoolhouse in those days, and I lived there during the week, only going home to Madisonburg on weekends. I borrowed John Lingle's shotgun one fall day during rabbit season, and I went into Hen Zerby's; his place was the next one after Piney Camp hunting lodge. He had a little black hunting dog, which had a good reputation as a rabbit hound, and I asked him if I could borrow it. In his thick Pennsylvania Dutch accent, he replied, 'You can borrow it, but you von't get any t'ing!'

"I took the dog and went up onto the Brown property, which is just west of the mountain cemetery. Many times, I found Craters' cows roaming here and returned them, so I was familiar with the place. Well, the dog kicked out a rabbit, but I shot at another one that I thought I saw in some mountain laurel along the road by a swamp.

I thought I had hit it, but when I went in and looked for it, I couldn't find a trace of him, dead or alive. I hunted some more after that, but I didn't see any more rabbits, or any other game for that matter, the rest of the afternoon, and when I returned his dog, old Zerby just laughed."[8]

Clarence Musser attributed the strange events of his ill-fated rabbit hunt to the imagination, but he also recalled that it was almost dark by the time he got back to the mountain schoolhouse that same day. I often thought of him winding his way back down the mountains that fall evening after the odd episode with the elusive rabbits, and I can't help but wonder if his pace picked up just a little as he noticed darkness creeping in around him.

In the Blue Mountains of Berks and Lehigh Counties, there was once a story about a hunter like rabbit-hunter Clarence Musser, but in this case, the nimrod went into the woods to hunt squirrels. He saw quite a few of the animals and fired one shot after another at them, but he later reported he "was unable to bring any down." Then he said he was surprised to see one particularly large squirrel he had not noticed before. He fired at it but missed it as well, but just afterward, he noticed "a little old grey man hiding behind the bole of a nearby tree."

The hunter immediately took a dime, which was still made of silver in those days instead of the copper-clad variety we have today, and loaded

8. Clarence Musser (born 1884), interviewed August 28, 1971 and November 21, 1971.

it into his gun while mumbling under his breath, "I'll show that thunder weather a thing or two!" He then fired his gun into the top of the tree, whereupon the little old man disappeared." Since silver bullets were thought to be the most effective way to kill a witch or bewitched animals, the story concludes by noting that "from then on the hunter shot without missing."[9]

Belief in stories like the preceding ones, and about bewitched game in general, was undoubtedly reinforced when people found the formulas for doing the bewitching printed on the pages of a book, especially one like *The Long Lost Friend*. In that book, John George Hohman, the widely accepted authority on such matters in those days, laid out many spells and counter-spells, including one to prevent someone from killing game.

According to him, it was easily accomplished by just reciting the following verse: "(Name of person), shoot whatever you please; shoot but hair and feathers with what you give to poor people. In the name of The Father, The Son, and the Holy Ghost."[10]

Perhaps people living around Hen Zerby or near others with similar reputations also recalled the fabled stories of little grey men of the woods when hunters spoke of the local game being hard to shoot or to find. Many folks probably found such supernatural tales to be a satisfactory explanation for the hunters' lack of success, but they might have done better if they had looked for other explanations as well. For instance, in Hen Zerby's case there may have indeed been a shortage of game in the area surrounding his homestead.

Remembered by some of his neighbors as "the nicest person you could ever live around," Zerby was also known as an avid hunter.[11] It's recalled, for example, that one fall day, while helping some neighbors butcher, Zerby and his son Jim heard some turkeys calling from the top of a nearby ridge. Zerby immediately declared their services at an end, stating that he wanted to track the birds down. With that, he and his son "dropped everything and went off hunting."[12]

---

9. Thomas R. Brendle and William S. Troxell, "Pennsylvania German Folk Tales, Legends, Once-upon-a-time Stories, Maxims, and Sayings," *Proceedings of the Pennsylvania German Society, Volume L*, 201.

10. John George Hohman, *Pow-Wows or The Long Lost Friend*, 62.

11. Clayton Auman (born 1885), recorded October 31, 1981.

12. Randall Steiger (born 1904), recorded May 4, 1988.

Dedicated hunters like the Zerbys could easily reduce the number of turkeys and other game animals in an area over some time, and, in fact, it was recalled that Hen Zerby himself shot thirteen turkeys during one year in particular. Individual harvests like this were perfectly legal in those times—in the days before game laws were enacted, strictly enforced, and accepted as something necessary for prudent wildlife management. Consequently, when looking back, it seems fair to say that although they were not exactly like the legendarily acclaimed little grey men of the woods that thwarted hunters' quests for game, mountaineers like Henry Zerby did manage, in their own way, to achieve somewhat the same results.

NOTE: There is an interesting account in the reminiscences of Philip Tome, pioneer hunter of north central Pennsylvania in the early 1800s, where he recalls an "unshootable buck" he and some companion hunters failed to down one hot July day along Pine Creek, in 1805. It undoubtedly would have provided reassurance for some that witches could indeed take the fire from a gun! Tome's account reads:

"Going up the creek about five miles, we commenced floating down and soon shot a deer, which we stowed away in the canoe. When we had gone a short distance further, two of us saw a deer in the stream, and both fired at the same time, but neither appeared to hit it. We reloaded and directed the man who was steering to run the canoe to the shore.

"We then stood on the shore, about thirty rods from the deer, and each fired eight shots at it, as rapidly as we could load, when our guns became so hot that we were compelled to stop. The steersman had been holding up the torch for us to see by, yet the position of the animal was the same as when we first observed.

"At each shot it had seemed to spring up, each time higher and higher, and dropping into the same spot. We now threw sticks at it to drive it away when it gave two or three leaps and suddenly disappeared. This affair may appear somewhat strange to the reader, as it did to me, but the facts are as I have stated and always appeared to me to be unaccountable."[13]

---

13. Philip Tome, *Pioneer Life or Thirty Years a Hunter*, 138.

CHAPTER 6

HAIRY JOHN

Near the eastern edge of Centre County, where its boundary line with Union County is defined, there is a natural gap or cut through the mountains that connects the villages of Woodward, Centre County, and Hartleton in Union County. This gloomy defile, popularly known as the Woodward Narrows, is always filled with somber shadows in some of its deeper glens and hollows, and even at midday on some days, the forest here is home only to whispering pines, restless oaks, and the soft murmur of Voneida Run as it courses through the cool mists of the dark forest.

Due to its lack of human habitation and infrequent traffic, the mountain pass often seems like one of those places where few people care to tarry and where time itself appears to have come to a standstill. However, despite its somber and melancholy atmosphere, this quaint little corner of woodland is surrounded by acres of state forest, and so it holds many attractions for the nature lover.

Like other state forest preserves, the mountain land that extends for miles around Woodward Narrows provides an ideal habitat for wild turkeys and deer, a fact that hasn't escaped the many hunters that are drawn here every hunting season. It's a scenic territory, typical of many of the beautiful woodlands preserved as state forest land here in Pennsylvania, and so this spot also appeals to hikers, campers, and picnickers who take advantage of its refreshing forest breezes, nature's air conditioning during the hottest days of summer. However, there is one other attraction here that has undoubtedly drawn the merely curious to this unique place for decades.

Along the northern side of Route 45, the state road that passes through the narrows, there was once a signboard here that advertised the little parklet as "Hairy John's State Park," but that park was eventually demoted due to lack of funding to "Hairy John's picnic area." Nonetheless, despite the demotion, the small rest stop's strange name was always guaranteed to cause even the most impassive travelers to take a second look as they passed. However, those who are inclined to wonder about such things will want to know more about this strange character named Hairy John, who he was and why this area is named after him.

It's an account that has never been formally recorded in any official biography, and it's not a tale that's remembered much at all today. However, the story has been preserved in local legends that still cling to this mini wilderness formed by the towering heights of Winkelblech, Sand, and Thick Mountains.

The site of Hairy John's park is located in the Bald Eagle State Forest of Centre and Union Counties, a picturesque region where many romantic and thrilling episodes occurred once upon a time. Narratives of panthers, wolves, Indians, ghosts, and witches were once quite plentiful here, but the story of Hairy John was probably always one of peoples' favorites.

It was undoubtedly often repeated around the cracker barrels of local country stores and beside the hearths of remote mountain cabins. Beside cozy inglenooks on cold winter evenings, children heard the tale from their parents and grandparents, passing it on to their children over the years, and so it has come down to us in this way today.

It has not really been that long ago that John Voneida could be found in his little cabin along the narrows that would later bear his name. Likewise, not too many decades ago, there were people still alive who could recall seeing the old hermit of the narrows come into the nearby village of Woodward to buy molasses, flour, and other staples. Sometimes, too, he would come just to pay a visit to his brother Henry, who lived at the foot of the *Rundkupf*, or Roundtop Mountain.

Roundtop Mountain towers over the town of Woodward like a dark and silent sentinel and can be seen from miles away when approaching the

John Voneida's Taufschein. This original "Taufschein" is typical of those kept by many Pennsylvania Dutch families prior to the twentieth century. This one for John Voneida has been preserved and handed down to succeeding generations by his descendants. Beautifully multi-colored "Frakturschriften" like these were commissioned from itinerant or local artists by families who wished to preserve a record of their child's birth.

hamlet. However, old Roundtop was not the only feature for which the town was once noted. In fact, the thing that really set Woodward apart from the other settlements around it at one time was the pleasant smell of wood smoke that came from the town's many wood-burning stoves.

Anyone entering the village around mealtime, even just seventy years ago, would immediately notice the pungent odor coming from the clouds of smoke that were reminders of an earlier time—a time when butchering, apple butter boiling, corn husking, and quaint mountain characters like Hairy John were part of everyday rural life here.

Although hardy mountaineer types of all kinds had passed through Woodward since 1818, when stage coaches traveling between Bellefonte and Northumberland stopped for rest and repast at Henry Roush's tavern in the Woodward Narrows, none of them seems to have made a lasting impression upon anyone. However, the hermit of the Narrows did, and stories about him were told and retold, including how his quiet entrances into the sleepy village of Woodward always were a signal for the children of the town to run and hide from the hairy little man.

Voneida's long hair and lengthy beard must have been intimidating to the youngsters, but it was probably the tales they had heard their parents tell about him that really made them afraid. For John Voneida's past was clouded by a dark secret, a terrible story that caused some to fear him.

Nasty rumors seemed to travel with the kindly recluse. There were insinuations that he had left his wife because of constant disagreements and other marital problems, abandoning her to live a solitary existence in the mountains. There were even harsher rumors that claimed that "he mistreated his wife, and then ran into the woods to live away from her"[1] or even that "he was accused of killing her."[2] But the diminutive recluse stoutly denied any such gossip, preferring instead to show people that he was a harmless and goodhearted person.

One of the ways the hermit was known for polishing his image was his penchant for offering food and drink to travelers passing by his remote cabin located in the lonely mountain pass near Woodward. Then others recalled that he even acted as sort of a wayside postmaster, allowing travelers to leave messages for other travelers at his forest home. Nevertheless, despite Voneida's best attempts, the rumors about him persisted; mainly because they were based upon true events.

Older folks who once knew the man related that he had originally come from nearby Nittany Valley, probably having lived around the little town of Jacksonville before settling down in the mountains above Woodward. These same oral traditions go on to state that while living in Jacksonville,

---

1. Rachael Krape (born 1902), recorded June 23, 1990.
2. Jean Voneida (born 1934), recorded November 13, 1982.

Where "Hairy John's" cabin once stood. His cabin is no longer standing, but the natural beauty of this spot is perhaps just as alluring today as it was to John Voneida when he built his log cabin along here in the 1860s or '70s. Hairy John's State Forest Picnic Area, near Woodward, Bald Eagle State Forest, Centre County.

Voneida was married to a young mountain lass named Susanna, who was the daughter of George Hoy of Madisonburg. The old legends don't say much more about her other than there was a belief that she was mentally unstable—or feeble-minded, as they would say in those times.

The old accounts claim that her mental state deteriorated to the point where her inner demons drove her to suicide and that one day, she hanged herself in a closet inside the Voneida's homestead. It was perfect material for the rumor mill since people in those days had little understanding of mental illnesses of any kind, and so tongues began to wag. Eventually, the rumor turned to slander, with some people saying Susanna had not committed suicide at all, that her husband had hung her himself.

Eventually, the children of the town, hearing their parents' accusations, began to taunt the bereaved widower whenever they saw him in the streets, and it was more than he could stand. He was eventually driven away, preferring a solitary life in the mountains to neighbors of any kind. Here, he took on the look of a typical recluse, letting his hair and his beard grow so long that people eventually began to refer to him by the nickname "Hairy John," which was to stay with him the rest of his life.[3]

---

3. Clarence Musser (born 1884), interviewed August 28, 1971, and November 21, 1971.

Voneida was apparently of a studious turn of mind because, according to the legends, he spent part of his time in the Woodward Narrows by writing a philosophy of some sort. It was thought that he devoted the last fourteen years of his life to his self-appointed task, but no one today seems to know much about his treatise or if he even actually wrote one. Perhaps with diligent searching, copies can be found in some of the larger libraries in the state, but they are probably quite rare.

The little hermit's *taufschein* or birth certificate, a beautiful piece of *fraktur* colorfully decorated with tulips, hearts, distelfinks, and other typical Pennsylvania Dutch motifs, has been preserved by Voneida descendants and can still be seen today. The date of birth on the certificate is almost indecipherable but is most likely November 27, 1815, or 1837. The certificate is entirely written in old-fashioned German script, with the names of the parents given as Johannes Von Neida and his wife Susannah.

Although his birth certificate still exists, John Voneida's gravesite may be harder to find. He is said to be buried in a cemetery near Madisonburg, Centre County, but the inscription on the tombstone may now be so well-weathered that it is almost indecipherable. Since historical facts are so sparse, the only other way we may hope to find any details about this strange character is to turn to the cloudy and unreliable stories of oral tradition, and one of these traditional tales recalls that John Voneida was known to be a determined deer hunter, exhibiting unusual persistence in bagging his quarry.

"One of the things I heard," recalled one present-day hunter, "and I don't know if it's true or not, but when he'd hunt deer and see the tracks, he'd just keep on 'em, day and night, until he'd finally get it!"[4]

A contemporary of Voneida's, who was also known for his determination when it came to tracking deer, was Joshua Roush of Woodward. More will be said about this hardy devotee of the chase in a future volume, but for now, it can be noted that Roush was famous for capturing deer live rather than killing them. It was this technique, however, that resulted in a little-known episode of the Woodward Narrows that relates how Roush and his captured deer disrupted John Voneida's quiet lifestyle one night.

Tales of Josh Roush's stamina and single-mindedness during the chase are still kept alive by his descendants, and one of their accounts tells of his

---

4. Harry Burd (born 1905), recorded May 27, 1988.

Hairy John's Pond and top of the wall from which the spring water flows. This everflowing mountain spring provided John Voneida with his water, and local Amish families still come here today to fill their jugs with cold fresh mountain water to provide drinking water for their families,

"pack of dogs that could, and did, trail a deer until it was so tired that the dogs could corner it and hold it until Josh could get it."[5] Live deer like this could be sold at zoos or game parks, and Roush's pack was trained to help capture the most outstanding specimens.

Just as a pack of determined wolves keeps chasing a deer until it can no longer run, Roush's dogs hounded a stag until it dropped. Once the deer was in this state, Roush could easily rope it and carry it back to his deer pens, which stood beside his home on the mountain back of Woodward. And so say the old legends, it was a deer just like this, one that Roush had captured alive, that resulted in a lively evening for Hairy John and his guest.

Josh and his frenzied pack would track a deer for miles, like John Voneida, following it over rugged mountain peaks, down into dark and mysterious ravines, and through tangled thickets of laurel bushes or rhododendron. Day and night, the chase would continue until either the deer was captured or it managed to throw the dogs off its scent by walking up a swift creek.

---

5. Dorothy Meyer (born 1915), letter to the author dated May 4, 1978; and telephone conversation on October 25, 1980.

Hairy John's Pond as it looks today. It overflows into a spillway when full, but when a drought period occurs the pond dries up.

Late one day, after following a particularly large buck for many miles, Roush and his pack cornered the stag on Winkelblech Mountain, just above the town of Woodward. Here the rugged nimrod rushed up to the winded deer and threw it down, bulldogging it like a rodeo cowboy. After tying the deer's legs together, Roush flung it over his shoulder and started for home.

The sun was sinking lower in the evening sky by this time, and soon, its last rays were barely visible over the solemn outlines of Shriner Mountain to the west. In a few minutes, it was dark, and the tired hunter decided he would see if he could stay at John Voneida's cabin for the night.

It was a haven from the panthers and wolves that still roamed the mountains at that time, and Roush knew the hermit would welcome him. Even though the wolves and mountain lions were becoming scarce, there were still enough of them around to arouse concerns in the mind of someone who was caught in the woods and far from home as darkness approached.

Just as Roush expected, the friendly hermit welcomed his wayward guest and told him that he and his hog-tied deer could spend the night safely inside the isolated cabin. The two men laid the deer in one corner of the place and after checking that the animal's feet were securely tied,

crawled into their beds and drifted off to sleep. But sometime in the middle
of the night the stag kicked long and hard enough that it managed to get
loose.

Half-crazy with fright, the confused animal began running around the
room. The building's other two occupants were rudely awakened by the
sounds of clattering pots and pans as they were knocked from tables and
pantry shelves by the frenzied deer. But somehow, the sleepy men managed
to recapture the animal and tie it up again, this time making extra sure it
could not escape. Whether they were able to get any more sleep that night
is anyone's guess.[6]

The adventure of the rampaging deer was not an episode that the fairer
sex would have appreciated, and so the incident probably occurred before
the time that another woman entered John Voneida's life and ended his
solitary existence. Eventually, his grief over his wife's suicide decreased to
the point where he once again longed for female companionship. The local
folk tales say that he finally did find a suitable companion to share his
lonely lifestyle, but they have very little else to say about this obscure person. It seems that not much was ever known about her.

Some say her name was Twila Montray, but this is not certain since her
origins seem lost. She may have been what was then disparagingly known
as a half-breed, the derogatory term used in those days for the offspring of
a union between an Indian woman and a settler.

In any case, it would appear that John and his female companion
found some happiness, at least for a while, there in their little mountain
retreat. However, Voneida's life seems to have been destined to be plagued
by tragedy. Tragic events led him to his peaceful existence in the Woodward
Narrows, and it was violence that ended it.

Perhaps the little hermit made some enemies because of the way he
lived or because of the way he always frightened local children. On the
other hand, maybe a few local miscreants were convinced that there was
a horde of cash hidden in the hermit's cabin. Whatever the case may be,
John Voneida apparently became a marked man in the eyes of a few jaded
individuals.

6. Dorothy Meyer (born 1915), letter to the author dated May 4, 1978; and telephone conversation on
October 25, 1980.

He must have seemed like easy prey to ruffians since he is remembered as being a small, thin man, and so it would seem certain that it was several cowardly thieves who set upon the harmless little hermit one day and beat him so badly that he fled the area. The old stories say that he clung to life for a while after his thrashing, but in the end, his injuries proved too severe, and he died from them. Apparently, he must have died in Madisonburg, for this is where his final resting place is said to be.

Twila Montray's fate is not as clear at this point, although some say she was also beaten to death by the same criminals that attacked her soul mate. If that is true, then it is no wonder that John Voneida failed to recover from his beating. His heart and his spirit were probably broken as well. But legends are kinder than history when it comes to describing the fate of Hairy John and his Twila.

The folktales about them indicate that John had always expressed a wish that his spirit would find a home in a beech tree when he died and that this is what happened. However, even though these same narratives don't say where any such beech tree exists today in the park, a few people have claimed that a commemorative one was planted on the site of the hermit's cabin when the park was dedicated. Details about Twila Montray's fate are just as sketchy, but some believe that her spirit is there yet today and swear that "her spirit haunts the Narrows."[7]

So, it would appear that if the old legends are accurate, the ghost of Twila Montray flits through the Woodward Narrows on peaceful summer nights when winds are low, the moon is full, and whippoorwills call from the depths of laurel thickets on Winkelblech Mountain. It sounds like such a cruel fate to be destined to haunt the Woodward Narrows for eternity, especially for someone who suffered such a terrible end to her own life. But there just may be a kinder and gentler ending to this tragic tale.

The notion that victims of violent deaths come back to haunt the scenes of their demise is a typical folktale motif found throughout the world. But in this case, some say Twila's ghost is here because it wants to be near the beech tree that holds the spirit of John Voneida. They prefer to believe that John Voneida will have his sweetheart near him for all time; their two spirits are inseparably bound forever. If they are correct, it would

7. Hugh Manchester (born 1925), recorded November 6, 1981.

Ghost Girl in the Woods. ShutterStock image. An image that struck a chord with me because I imagined it to be similar to what the ghost girl in the Woodward Narrows, if there is one, might look like when it chooses to appear to unsuspecting nighttime motorists!

then appear that legend has picked up where life, in its harshness, wrote an unsatisfactory ending.

EPILOGUE: One fall evening about thirty years ago, a young couple was driving through the Woodward Narrows and had an experience that some might say substantiates the Twila Montray ghost story convincingly. It was about 9:30 PM, and they remember the night as being clear and beautiful, with no fog to diffuse the car's headlights. Their vehicle was heading west, towards the little village of Woodward, and they had just passed through Hairy John's Park about two miles back when suddenly, and seemingly out of nowhere, something strange appeared on the road ahead.

"It looked more like fog, but it was definitely moving," explained the man who was driving at the time. "It wasn't a bright patch, but it was something, and it was in motion. As soon as we got up there, it was in motion, left to right, almost as if it was going to cross the road. And during that time, we passed through it, and it was almost as if we stood still for a second."

"We went right through it, and it wasn't fog," continued the man's wife. "We really thought we were hitting something. I couldn't make out any shape like a head, a person, or a deer, or anything like that, but there was a mass of something. It was big, bigger than a deer, and it seemed like an image of a person. I grabbed the dashboard and screamed, and he hit the brakes and was stopping!"

"I thought I hit a deer, but there was no obvious bump or anything like that," interjected the husband. "I felt like there was definitely something there and that there should've been a thump or a bump, or like we hit something, but it was just kind of like a swoosh! It almost seemed as though the car stalled or something.

"I said, 'Let me get out and look.' I checked the car, and there was nothing; I walked back around and looked there and on the road, and there was nothing! But when I was walking back there, I felt creepy! I mean it was obvious there is something wrong here, and I don't know what it is! I got back in, and I said, 'That was really weird!' It was almost as if maybe we drove through a ghost or something like that!"[8]

---

8. Mr. and Mrs. Jake Fryer, recorded September 13, 1997.

CHAPTER 7

TOOTH AND CLAW

In his interesting history of northwestern Pennsylvania, published in 1905, William J. McKnight outlines some pertinent facts about the mountain lions that were once so prevalent throughout all of the Keystone State. McKnight claims that these magnificent beasts, also referred to as panthers in the old days, were "fully as strong as a bear, but were rather cowardly"[1]—an assessment not entirely in concert with stories about panther attacks that have sometimes come down to us via the highways of oral tradition, and which, in some cases, have even been recorded in other history books.

Certainly, if all the verbally preserved episodes are also accepted as having some legitimate truths behind them, rather than being rejected merely because they do not appear in some weighty leather-bound volume of official history, it is easy to conclude that, under the right conditions, panthers are not reduced to scared rabbits when encountering a man. In fact, just the opposite is true if someone is unfortunate enough to cross the path of a hungry lion with a fresh kill or to stumble upon a mother with newborn cubs. As one early historian has noted, "Although the panther did not usually attack humans, this could not be accepted with any degree of certainty, especially if it were a female nursing a litter of cubs."[2]

---

1. William J. McKnight, *Pioneer Outline History of Northwestern Pennsylvania*, 174.
2. J. Marvin Lee, "King of the Pennsylvania Forests," *Centre County Heritage, Volume 1, 1956, through Volume XI, 1975*, 66.

Among the things guaranteed to turn a mountain lion from a placid-looking pussycat into a raging beast are the two situations just mentioned, and there once were undoubtedly many such stories that told of men being attacked for one of these two reasons. Tales like this are hard to come by today, except for those recorded in the many county histories that are kept in libraries, but a few of these stories, and some accounts that have never been set down in print before, are included in this essay just to give the reader an idea of how rough and ready the early settlers of these timeworn mountains must have been. And there is probably no better way to begin than to tell a story of old Sam Askey, that great panther hunter of Snow Shoe, Centre County.

Sam Askey's reputation as a slayer of many Pennsylvania panthers and wolves was well established throughout northern Centre and western Clinton County at one time, but those who counted him as a personal friend and who had heard him relate some of his hunting escapades claimed Askey's life would "compare with that of Daniel Boone or David Crockett."[3]

Said to have been the slayer of sixty-four panthers and ninety-eight wolves just while living at Snow Shoe, Askey, during his lifetime of hunting, had several hand-to-hand encounters with panthers and bore the scars of these fights with him to his grave. The old hunter was, in his old age, fond of recalling these episodes to avid listeners, and he undoubtedly could tell a thrilling story about each of the bodily scars that he had gotten as a result of a panther attack. One such tale, in particular, was about the day he was ambushed by a lioness on Big Moshannon Mountain.

Askey, who died in 1857 at the ripe old age of eighty-one, was especially fond of hunting on the Allegheny Mountains above Snow Shoe in that section of wild and untamed forest where the Big and Little Moshannon Creeks wind their way down to the West Branch of the mighty Susquehanna River.

Spring, summer, winter, or fall, Askey could be found on these ragged slopes searching for deer, panthers, bears, or wolves to add to his long list of hunting trophies. However, it was during one cold winter day that the mighty hunter had one of his most unforgettable hand-to-hand fights with a panther.

---

3. John Blair Linn, *History of Centre and Clinton Counties*, 422.

A Pennsylvania Mountian Lion. Photo taken in March of 2023 on Big Poe Mountain along the Millheim / Siglerville Pike. The photo is very blurry, perhaps because the photographer's hand were shaking when he took the photo at a somewhat close range! The color version of the photo leaves no doubt that this is indeed a mountain lion. (Photo courtesy of Mitchel Schaeffer.)

A particularly good tracking snow had just fallen the night before, and Askey decided to take one of his best dogs hunting. It wasn't long before he found fresh tracks somewhere on the mountains between the two Moshannon creeks. Since he was on an especially difficult spot on the ridge, Askey decided to tether his dog to his body so as to keep the animal under control while he tried to follow the panther's tracks up the steep slope. Thinking he would release the dog once the hiking became easier, the cagy hunter finally made it to the top of the peak he called the Big Moshannon Hill.

After attaining the brow of the ridge, the hunter and the little cur tethered to him approached a large rock that projected out over the trail. Just as they passed in front of the outcrop, a panther that lay concealed in an opening under it pounced upon the dog. The result was a writhing tangle of man, canine, and beast all rolling down the hill, with, in Askey's words, "sometimes the panther uppermost, sometimes the dog, and sometimes myself."[4]

4. John Blair Linn, *History of Centre and Clinton Counties*, 422.

Since the dog was tied to him with a slipknot, Askey managed to free himself, but the panther and dog rolled all the way down to the bottom of the slope, locked in a death struggle while growling and snarling at each other the whole time. When the two animals reached level ground, the panther disengaged itself from the dog and raced up the nearest tree.

This just gave Askey time enough to retrieve his gun, which had fallen out of his grasp while he was rolling down the hill. Finding his rifle to be in good shape, the determined hunter spotted the panther up in the tree and brought the beast down with one well-directed shot.

Close inspection of the panther revealed that it was a female that had been nursing cubs, and so the fearless nimrod decided he would make a firsthand inspection of the den under the rock from which the attack had come. The opening was just big enough to allow him to enter, so he carefully squeezed into the dark hole, where, much as he had expected, he found four small panther cubs hiding in the den.

Each was about the size of a common house cat. Askey found them to be about as friendly as tame felines and certainly friendlier than their mother. Their docile nature impressed the old hunter so much that he wrote about them in his hunting diary, noting that "after handling them for a short time, they fondled on me like young kittens."[5]

Nonetheless, the practical hunter and hardened veteran of countless chases had no intention of keeping the furry little bundles as pets. He must have killed them too, for he would later relate that the day's work had been hard, and the bounties he received for the panthers' pelts were not enough to compensate him for the injuries that had been inflicted upon his dog. The faithful canine was permanently disabled by its terrible struggle with the mother panther and, said Askey, "was of no use to me afterward."[6]

Sam Askey was certainly not the only one who had a hair-raising encounter with aggressive panthers here in Pennsylvania during the 1800s and early 1900s, if an incident in Blackmans' *History of Susquehanna County*, published in 1872, can be believed.

In 1806, according to Blackman's account, a man named Asa Bradley was building a log cabin in the unsettled wilderness around what was to

---

5. Ibid.
6. Ibid.

become the present-day town of New Milford, but progress was slow, and so a nearby pioneer family invited Bradley, his wife, and his children to stay with them until the Bradley homestead was finished.

They stayed there for a while but grew anxious to be in their place, so the Bradleys finally decided to move into it, even though it was still only partially completed; the walls and the roof were in place, but there was no front door. Nonetheless, it was a home, and they would no longer have to impose upon their gracious hosts any longer. So, they hung a blanket over the opening where a front door would eventually be placed and moved into their new log cabin.

Sometime during their first night in the cabin, the family was awakened by loud squeals which came from a pig they had placed in a pen attached to the house. Although concerned, they decided not to investigate the sounds that night since the squealing eventually died away, but the next morning, when they went outside, they discovered their pig was gone. After a brief search, they found the hog not too far from the cabin.

The little porker had been partly devoured, and tracks all around the pigpen proved that the culprit was a panther. The Bradleys counted themselves lucky, despite the loss of their prized hog, for upon thinking about the matter, they realized that had the pig not been there for the panther's meal, then there would have been nothing that would have prevented the ravenous beast from entering their house, attacking them, and dining upon them.[7]

Although the Bradleys were spared the horrors of a full-fledged panther attack, and so did not have to fend off the teeth and claws of such an intimidating beast, others were not so fortunate over the years. Older folks around Blackwell, Tioga County, for example, still remember hearing stories when they were younger about a local miner who was attacked and killed by a panther in earlier times.

Details of the story seem to have been lost over the years, and this is what has probably happened to many other similar accounts as decades have passed. However, this has not always been the case, as exemplified by one striking episode from Lycoming County that occurred around the turn of the twentieth century.

---

7. Emily C. Blackman, *History of Susquehanna County, Pennsylvania,* 151.

Many folks traveling north out of Salladasburg on Route 287 may never have paid much attention to a large stone monument that sits on the right side of the highway just after they've passed through English Center. People's eyes are naturally drawn instead to the inviting appearance of a neatly kept bed and breakfast lodge that sits further back from the road some distance behind the solitary rock. However, if a closer look is taken at the stone, the observer will note that fastened to it is a plaque that has an inscription engraved upon its surface.

The plaque has been exposed to the elements for so long that its black surface has weathered down in spots to the bare metal of a bronze shade, producing an effect that reminds you of a leopard's skin. Then, too, if the inscription is read, the reader will be surprised to learn that the commemorative plaque was placed there in memory of an incident involving one of the leopard's distant cousins.

The English Center marker is unique since it may be the only one in Pennsylvania that preserves the memory of a man being killed by one of the state's mountain lions. Its inscription recalls the event as follows:

> In memory of Dr. Frederick Reinwald
> Dr. Reinwald was killed by a panther at Black's Creek,
> four miles northeast of this point, December 22, 1896,
> while on his way to visit a patient. An unusual example
> of the fortitude of pioneer physicians and the hazards
> faced in the performance of their duties.

This was undoubtedly an attack that actually happened upon an unfortunate doctor whose sense of duty was stronger than his concerns for his safety. Such a man deserves to be remembered, and so it's no surprise that local legends supply a few additional details about his demise.

"He went out toward Liberty [Tioga County] with his horse and buggy to take care of some sick people, and he was killed by a black panther," offered one older native of the area. "That's the only one I ever heard about around here. I suppose the poor cat was hungry!"[8]

---

8. Howard Heggenstaller (born 1920), recorded November 16, 1989.

So, although the color of the panther was probably tawny, the typical color of Pennsylvania mountain lions, instead of black, the good doctor's memory also lives on in the folktales of Lycoming County. The unfortunate thing is that the Lycoming County physician was just in the wrong place at the wrong time and without a chance to defend himself. However, in most cases, the outcome of an encounter between humans and the big cats called panthers rarely ended up with the mountain lions being victorious; a statement which is supported by another panther story from Centre County, which tells of a mountain lion that attacked a man and paid the ultimate price for it. However, in this case, it appears that, in the end, the panther eluded his killer after all.

"There was supposed to be a panther roaming the woods right close by here," recalled the valley native in a thick Pennsylvania Dutch accent as he was telling me the tales of the olden days one fine spring afternoon in 1989. "Oh, that was before I was born," continued the seventy-seven-year-old. "I heard about it from a neighbor when I was a kid. Samuel Styers was an old white-haired man, close to eighty years old, and he used to come out there and visit us. I didn't put too much stock in what he said because he was known as a big storyteller and a liar, but he told us that he had a son who was attacked by a panther one night.

"Later on, he went out, and he shot this panther along Woodward Mountain here. I always knew the names of the gaps in the mountain. Haines Gap is the one out here, and the break in the mountain where our reservoir is, is called Young's Gap. And this panther was supposed to be making its home in Young's Gap and traveling along the mountain towards Coburn.

"I was born in 1912, and I was about fifteen years old, I guess, when old man Styers told me about that. So, it must've been back in the 1800s when he shot it. He wanted it mounted, but he said he never had enough money to do it. He skinned it and gave it to a taxidermist, and the taxidermist mounted it, but they couldn't pay for it, so the taxidermist kept it."[9]

Perhaps it's just as well that the Styers' panther disappeared. Even stuffed ones seemed too lifelike at times for some people who weren't too sure about those teeth and claws that still looked threatening on the motionless

---

9. Ray Stover (born 1912), recorded May 19, 1989.

effigies. Perhaps it was this uncertainty that gave birth to the old idea that at night, stuffed panthers could come back to life and roam the forests once again, just like they did when they were alive.

Such superstitions were also probably reinforced by the fact that dogs were intimidated by these grotesque figures. A record of one such incident is preserved in the historical annals of Susquehanna County, where it's recalled that during the early 1800s in Jackson Township, there was a social gathering of some of the old pioneers of that area.

Samuel Ard, who hosted the event, livened up the proceedings by exhibiting a stuffed panther, which was fully nine feet in length from the tip of its tail to the end of its nose. The taxidermist who had prepared the effigy had been so skillful that it was said that the result "looked enough like life to frighten even dogs."[10]

It probably frightened the women too, and no doubt it raised fears in many, women and men alike, that it would draw other panthers to it. Not something anyone who lived in those times would have wished for—particularly when it can surely be said that one of the credos of those days was that "the only good panther is a dead panther."

---

10. Albert M. Rung, *Rung's Chronicles of Pennsylvania History*, 91.

CHAPTER 8

GUARDIAN OF THE TRAIL

B efore it was known as Pennsylvania's Black Forest, the region of northern Pennsylvania now comprised of most of Potter and Tioga counties was called the Forbidden Land by the first pioneers that ventured into what was then an area known only to the Indians and to the wild creatures that roamed through it at will. The story behind this unusual name is documented somewhat in the early historical records of the region, but there is a legendary component to the name's origin as well.

However, this is a part of the story that has almost been forgotten over the years but which deserves to be re-explored, not only to document once again the injustices that were once heaped upon the rightful owners of the land but also to find the possible source of one more ghost tale from the deep woods.

While William Penn, that benevolent founder of Pennsylvania, was alive, the Indians here were assured of fair treatment and kind respect. Rather than confiscate Native American lands outright, like the Puritans of New England or the settlers of North Carolina, Penn insisted on paying the Indians a fair price for it. In fact, there was once a story told about Penn that preserves the popular conception, undoubtedly both then and now, of what type of man he was when dealing with Native Americans.

It relates that King Charles of England once told the little Quaker that the land he had given him in the New World was England's by right of discovery.

Guardian of the Blue Mountains. Serving as another reminder of the state's earliest inhabitants, who left their own colorful imprint upon the face of Pennsylvania's mountains, valleys, and rivers, this dark countenance frowns down upon the village of Dauphin, from Second Mountain, Dauphin County. It gives an impression that it perhaps is brooding over how the rightful owners of this land were unjustly displaced by the white man. Photo courtesy of Ernie Schaeffer. See the chapter titled "Cast into Stone" for more Indian "faces" and tales about them.

"Well," replied Penn, "just suppose a canoe full of savages should by some accident discover Great Britain. Would you vacate or sell?"[11]

---

11. Thomas L. Montgomery, editor, *Frontier Forts of Pennsylvania, Volume I*, vii.

So unusual was this attitude in those days that one student of the times, alluding to the Quaker policy of refusing to utter an oath, either judicially or profanely, described Penn's "Great Treaty" with the Indians at Philadelphia in 1682 as "the only treaty never sworn to and never broken."[12]

However, once the man the Indians called "Brother Ones"[13] died, his policies toward them died as well, thereby setting the stage for the terrible Indian wars that reddened the state's soil with the blood of colonists and Indians alike.

The litany of broken promises and fraudulent agreements that were inflicted upon the Indians of Pennsylvania after William Penn died would fill volumes. Sometimes, settlers were granted warrants to lands never purchased from the Indians, and even when purchases were made, they were often done dishonestly.

Probably the most famous of all such deceptions was the notorious Walking Purchase of 1737 when it was agreed by the Delaware Indians living in Pennsylvania at that time that a purchase boundary would be limited by how far a man could walk in a day and a half.

Government officials, determined to grab as much land as they could, hired athletes in top condition and instructed them to run as fast as they could instead of walking at the normal pace expected by the Indians. When the walkers took off at a sprint, the on-looking Delawares shouted in protest, but their shouts were ignored, and at the end of the designated day and a half, the territory covered was twice what the Indians had expected it would be.

"No sit down to smoke, no shoot a squirrel, but lun, lun, lun all day long!"[14] was the way one brave—'R'-less as the other Delaware Indians until they fully learned how to pronounce English—described the actions of the men who had covered the territory. But this protest was just as feeble as another made by an Iroquois chieftain in 1742 who, protesting that squatters were settling on unsold Pennsylvania Indian lands daily, complained that they also "spoil our hunting."[15]

---

12. C. Hale Sipe, *The Indian Chiefs of Pennsylvania*, 60-63.
13. Ibid.
14. John T. Faris, *Seeing Pennsylvania*, 261.
15. Lewis Cass Aldrich, *History of Clearfield County, Pennsylvania*, 459.

Eventually, the attraction of trinkets and hardware no longer fascinated the Indians enough to persuade them to sell what they seemed to have thought were merely the hunting rights to their lands. In the end, if an honest accounting were done, the amount the Indians received per acre of Pennsylvania territory was trivial, even for those days. Shamefully, it has been estimated the actual value of the goods used to buy Indian lands, items like guns, coats, blankets, needles, pipes, shoes, knives, hatchets, scissors, combs, tin pots, and looking glasses, would probably come to less than a cent per acre.

Gradually some Indians began to see what was happening to their land and culture, much like the brave that one day sat down on a log beside Conrad Weiser, the Penns' highly respected Indian agent, and began to crowd him off of it. After several annoying nudges from the Indian, Weiser asked for an explanation.

"This," said the young warrior, "is what the whites did to the Indians. They lighted unbidden on our lands. We moved on. They followed. We still moved, and they still followed. We are moving onward now, and they are following after. I will not push you from the log entirely, but will your people cease their crowding ere we roll into the waters?"[16]

As time wore on the Indians became more and more protective of their real estate, particularly that which was strategically important to them militarily; and of all the Indian trails that once existed in Pennsylvania, there was one that the Iroquois Confederacy considered especially important. This was the trail known as the Forbidden Path because the Iroquois Six Nations Confederacy declared that no settler would ever set foot upon it.

Also sometimes known as the Tioga Path, the trail was the so-called backdoor to the Iroquois country. Skirting the southern boundaries of the Six Nations' tribal lands, this famous trail, also known accurately as the warriors' path, ran from present-day Tioga, Pennsylvania, through Painted Post and Salamanca, New York, eventually swinging back down into Pennsylvania, where it passed through Genesee and then back into New York State.

A trail of such strategic importance could not be left unguarded, so the Iroquois Confederacy designated the Seneca Nation around Salamanca,

16. John F. Meginness, *Otzinachson*, 127.

New York, to be their "Keepers of the Western Door."[17] Even peaceful Moravian missionaries, often the first Europeans to interact with many Indians, were barred from the protected pathway. One such Knight of the Cross found this to be the case one day in 1767 when a Seneca chief discovered him on the roadway.

The chief demanded how he thought he could use "such an unfrequented road, which is no road for whites, and on which no white man has ever come?"[18] Finding after this that the Indians he came to teach were "not at all friendly to the cause of the Gospel," the devout man of God gave up his work here as a lost cause and went west to find other souls that needed saving.[19]

It was the Indians' careful policing of the Forbidden Path that led the early settlers to call the entire area it passed through the Forbidden Land, a name that was eventually forgotten after the lands were purchased from the Indians near the end of the eighteenth century. However, the fact remains that this section of the state was one of the last to be explored and one of the last to be settled, and that is perhaps why the old legend that came to be placed here has lasted so long.

Until now, much of what's been covered in this essay may be a lot of dry history to most folks, but it has been necessary to cover it all in order to discover the origins of a ghostly tale that has been told and retold for over two hundred years—a legend which still clings to the Forbidden Land because it's preserved in the minds of the area's old folks, who can still reach back into their memories to recall the story of the mysterious "Guardian of the Trail."

"There's a lake up there, over in the Forbidden Forest; the only lake, I guess, that Potter County has," recalled the Tioga County farmer who claimed he had heard the story from an aged Seneca Indian. "Rose Lake, I think it is. Well, I don't know, the white man just never traveled through it. According to the French missionaries who were here with the Indians, they didn't travel through it; they went around it.

"Well, I can't give you it all, but the ghost of an Indian warrior comes out of the lake to keep people from traveling the trail through the Forbidden

17. Paul A. W. Wallace, *Indian Paths of Pennsylvania*, 46.
18. Ibid., 47.
19. Ibid., 48.

Indian re-enactors at Old Fort Bedford. Taken by the author at a reenactment of the Battle of Bushy Run held at Old Fort Bedford, Bedford Historic Site, Bedford County, in August of 2010. These "Indians" accurately portrayed what Indian "guardians of the Forbidden Land Trail" must have looked like.

Land. The Indians talked about the ghost guarding the trail so that no white man could pass through. That's the gist of it."[20]

After pondering the story for a while, the farmer seemed to think it wasn't complete without some sort of explanation.

"Why would they put a ghost story out?" he wondered and then ended his tale with a final thought that is most likely the best explanation anyone can derive. "I think they used that to kinda scare the early whites,"[21] he reasoned, and he's probably right.

Due to the early colonists' unquenchable thirst for their land and riches, the people once known derisively as the red race certainly had good reasons for wanting to keep the white ones away from Indian lands. Initially, it had probably seemed, to both Europeans and Indians alike, that there would be more than enough space for all. The mountains and ridges of Pennsylvania

---

20. Howard Heggenstaller (born 1920), recorded November 16, 1989.
21. Ibid.

must have appeared to extend on forever to anyone gazing upon them for the first time in those days, and the Indians also must have regarded them in the same way, their name for the Allegheny Mountains being *Tyannuntas-acta* or The Endless Hills.[22] However, the settlers were certainly no less awed by what also appeared to them to be a limitless wilderness.

Through the greater part of the 1700s, Pennsylvania was almost nothing but forest, and a popular expression of the time was that "a squirrel could make its way from Philadelphia to Pittsburgh without ever leaving the trees!"[23] With such a forested expanse, it is not surprising that some sections of the state may have been harder to settle than others, but then the abundance of squirrels in some places could have contributed to the lack of settlements as well. One such place may have been Clearfield County, and the other may have been the Forbidden Land.

Some historians indicate that the Indians avoided the Clearfield area for a number of reasons. The waterways through here were not navigable to any great extent, and so walking was the only way to pass through the region. However, during those early days, there were a large number of wolves and panthers that made their homes here, making a journey by foot unduly hazardous. There was also a large rattlesnake population in this neighborhood because they thrived upon the huge numbers of squirrels that were drawn here by the abundance of nuts and berries that grew profusely on many bushes and trees.

Even by 1840, Clearfield County was still only partially settled, its population estimated to be just five people per square mile. But after the lumbermen came and cleared the forest away at the turn of the century, nuts and berries didn't grow as profusely anymore. As a result, without the food supply to sustain their former levels, the squirrel and rattler populations declined accordingly.

Similar to Clearfield County, the Forbidden Land section was tamed slowly, too, not only because the Indians once restricted access to this part of Penn's Wood but probably also because the wild animals that lurked here made it a forbidding place to be. But even these deterrents were not enough to keep the settlers away, and the Indians must have realized that something more was needed to accomplish this.

---

22. Paul A. W. Wallace, *Indian Paths of Pennsylvania*, 4.
23. William Ecenbarger, "Penn's Sylvania," *APPRISE* magazine, April 1989.

Their story about the ghostly guardian of the Forbidden Trail may have been the Indians' last desperate attempt to protect their native land. And, like a lot of legends, there may have even been some real episode upon which they based the story. There just may have been a warrior at one time, for example, who said that he would guard the Indians' lands, even after he was dead.

If European legends can be used as a guide, then this motif of eternal purgatory is not unusual; it is the basis for a number of famous legends, including that of "The Wandering Jew" and "The Flying Dutchman." So, if there ever was an Indian that uttered such an oath, then maybe he inspired others to recommit themselves to protecting the lands of their ancestors, and one such man does seem to have existed.

Around 1856, General Thomas Kane, who was the founder of Kane, McKean County, built a small log cabin of beech and maple logs on what was later to be the site of Kane, the town named after him. The Colonel used the place as a hunting camp, but in those days, a hunting camp was kept open for anyone's use when the owner wasn't there. Consequently, General Kane, who believed the Indians, as original occupants of the country, had a moral right to the land, always kept his camp open for Jim Jacobs, an aged Seneca Indian who seemed to be an aimless drifter.

Although his purpose for being around was not clear, it was thought that Jacobs was placed here by the Seneca "to visit various places where the treasure was hidden, and to see if it was endangered by the encroachments of whites or if it was uncovered by fire and windfall."[24] Perhaps Jim Jacobs was carrying on an old Indian tradition which was the basis for the guardian legend. On the other hand, maybe the settlers just made assumptions about his duties.

Knowing that there were silver deposits here, the whereabouts of which were thought to be known only by the Indians, settlers were always trying to find a way to discover them. They may have thought that Jim Jacobs was around to insure that the deposits of precious metals stayed hidden. Whatever the truth may be, it's interesting to see that the settlers also thought that there were watchmen assigned to this area by the Indians. Perhaps Jim Jacobs was the last of many guardians of the trail.

---

24. J. E. Henretta, *Kane and the Upper Allegheny*, 106.

Not a typical Pennsylvania Indian shelter. This depiction of an Indian wigwam or teepee appeared in Harper's Encyclopedia of United States History (vol. 10), New York, NY: Harper and Brothers, 1912, Benson John Lossing, ed. It is not, however, an accurate representation of a typical dwelling of Eastern Woodland Native Americans who lived in Pennsylvania during the 18th century. They did not live in teepees. but constructed bark huts which were conical-shaped structures covered with bark rather than with the animal hides that the Plains Indians used on their teepees. Eastern Indians also lived in larger dwellings they called "longhouses" as well as in log cabins.

Note: If any ghosts are guarding the Forbidden Land of the Indians, they must be mournful ones because they failed in their assigned task. In 1779, General John Sullivan and a huge contingent of Continental soldiers used the Forbidden Path to invade the Iroquois country and lay waste to its many Indian towns and settlements. It was a defeat from which the Indians never recovered. (See the story titled "Burned at the Stake," which appears in the author's *Pennsylvania Fireside Tales Volume 2* in this series of Pennsylvania mountain legends, for an interesting legend associated with this historic march and invasion).

CHAPTER 9

THAR'S GOLD IN THEM THAR HILLS

The phrase "Thar's gold in them thar hills" has perhaps been over-used in many forms of popular entertainment over the years, but there really are gold and silver treasures to be found in the mountains of Pennsylvania if our legends are to be believed. Tales of hidden caches of silver and gold are common in many different sections of Pennsylvania, but the state's Northern Tier counties, the former Black Forest region of Pennsylvania, seems to have more than its share of such stories.

There are at least three accounts of fabulous riches waiting to be found in the forests of the Northern Tier and probably even more sagas than that if the matter were pursued. However, other parts of the state have produced similar legends as well, and it should prove interesting to take a look at all of them.

One of the more popular Black Forest mysteries claims that over a million dollars' worth of silver bars was buried near Keating Summit, McKean County, during the War of 1812. This treasure, according to the old legend, was salvaged by the British from the wreck of a Spanish galleon in the Bahamas. Deciding that it would be unsafe to stash the treasure horde in that volatile part of the world, King George III's forces instead concluded that they needed to ship it to a safe English port in North America.

To make that trip, they recruited a local seaman who held the same nickname, but not the same infamous reputation, as Edward Teach, the notorious English pirate known as Captain Blackbeard, who, a hundred years earlier, had terrorized the West Indies and eastern coast of the American colonies.

There were not many buccaneers that could claim the notoriety that Captain Teach achieved in the heyday of pirate ships. Exploits of the pirate with the luxuriant black beard were so well known in the early 1700s that the name Blackbeard became synonymous with piracy, and Teach undoubtedly inspired others to take up a similar way of life. At the very least, it seems that even as long as a hundred years after Teach died in 1718, the thrill of piracy on the high seas still held an appeal for certain individuals.

During the War of 1812, for example, there were seamen who, at the behest of the American government, were given the authority to raid British ships; the intent of these forays was disruption of the British war effort against the American colonies. As a reward for their efforts, the privateers, as they became known, could keep anything of value they confiscated.

Bars of pure silver would have been a prize catch for any enterprising privateer, and so any British ship hauling such a treasure through American waters in 1812 would probably want to spend as little time at sea as possible. If so, then the existence of privateers around that time could explain why the McKean County legend goes on to state that Captain Blackbeard decided he would have better luck getting the salvaged silver bars into British hands if he were to dock at the port of Baltimore and haul the silver overland.

Determined to deliver the silver booty to British officials at any cost and afraid to return with the loot to England because of a Napoleonic blockade of the British Isles during that time, Blackbeard headed for Baltimore. After laying anchor there, he fitted out an expedition that was to follow the Susquehanna and Sinnemahoning Rivers northward until it reached the British-controlled territories of New York. It was to be a trip, if such a trip was ever made, that a seaman like Blackbeard would never forget.

A sailor who had never experienced the difficulties of backwoods travel in those days would have been totally unprepared for the superhuman effort required to transport wagonloads of heavy silver bars over narrow mountain roads that were hardly worthy of the name. Any such journey would have taken many days of struggling through thickly forested valleys, slogging

A an old-time pirate chest. Although there are hidden treasures supposedly waiting to be found in our Pennsylvania mountains, they are not likely to be stashed in a chest like this!

around or through mosquito-infested swamps, and straining to get over high ridges that would have seemed like obstacles placed there by the devil himself. None of these challenges would be like anything a veteran seaman had ever encountered during his many years at sea, and so this is probably why the legend claims that Blackbeard never completed his trip.

Once again, the tale takes up the thread by stating that the struggling expedition managed to get as far as where Renovo, Clinton County, sits today, and then from there, it took the twenty-three-mile portage to the famous Canoe Place of the Indians, which today is known as Port Allegany. Here, Blackbeard, physically exhausted and uncertain of his chances of completing his mission, is said to have given up the attempt, deciding instead to bury the silver near an old salt lick that was a popular gathering spot for the many elk that inhabited the area.

Here, the treasure was hidden, but when he came back for it later, the unfortunate Blackbeard was thwarted. Dense groves of hawthorns with their prickly spurs and thick stands of mountain laurel that darkened the forest floor made it impossible to discern the landmarks that marked the spot where the bars were buried, and it's held by many today that those same bars still lie hidden somewhere in the wolf-haunted forests of McKean County.

Not to be outdone by its neighbor to the west, Potter County has two treasure stories that are just as appealing as McKean County's legend of the silver bars. The first Potter County legend describes another fortune in silver that is hidden near Inez, on that piece of territory locals refer to as The Black Diamond. This silver, so claims the legend, was buried there by the Jesuits, those early missionaries who oftentimes accompanied French traders on their travels and who the historian Sipe has described as "true Knights of the Cross."[1]

"Two French traders and a Jesuit were gonna take a shipment of silver back up the Genessee," claimed one Potter County man who had heard the legend years ago. "They had got it off the Indians down here at the Tiadaghton trading post and were taking it because the French government in Canada wanted the silver. The party was waylaid by bandits, so I understand, but, as the story goes, they had buried the silver beforehand. That's right over the hill from my house here, at Inez—The Black Diamond. But I imagine that there's been a million dollars spent looking for the damn thing! Yeah, it's an old story."[2]

Whenever treasure is mentioned, people tend to think not only of silver but also of gold, its metallic cousin, and a second Potter County legend tells of a fortune in gold that is said to be buried near Borie in Summit Township. Near here, says the popular tale, a party of French-Canadian voyageurs and priests decided to hide several kegs of gold coins they were transporting from New Orleans to Montreal sometime in the 1690s. Wary of and alarmed by sightings of the warlike Seneca Indians, whose territory they were passing through, the voyageurs resorted to the same strategy as that followed by McKean County's Blackbeard.

Accordingly, they buried the gold near a large rock, marking the spot and noting local landmarks so they could find their treasure when they returned for it later. But according to the legend, they never made it back,

1. C. Hale Sipe, *The Indian Chiefs of Pennsylvania*, 108.
2. Howard Heggenstaller (born 1920), recorded November 16, 1989.

and the gold coins are still there, waiting for someone to uncover them. However, the legend also states that carved onto a large rock near where the coins are buried is the sign left by the Frenchmen so they could easily find them.

The mark they chose was a cross, and the Cross on the Rock, as it came to be known, was once a familiar landmark in the Borie area. No one knows where that landmark is today; others say it was destroyed when the railroad laid its lines through here.

However intriguing the tale of the voyageurs' gold may be, it has never achieved the popularity nor spurred the quests that another Northern Tier legend of lost gold has evoked. By far, the most famous fortune of the Northern Tier region is that of the wagonload of gold bullion that unaccountably disappeared one June day in 1863.

The tale of this lost gold shipment has probably created more weekend treasure hunters in Pennsylvania than all the state's other treasure stories combined. The legend has been kept alive over one hundred years by the residents of Elk and Cameron Counties, who remember the fuss the incident caused during the Civil War and who have seen a steady stream of fortune seekers flow into the area ever since.

"An army force was shipping gold by mule train from Pittsburgh, up around by Saint Marys, and then down the Susquehanna during the Civil War," recalled the Potter County native who had heard the tale from the time he was a boy. "It come up out of Pittsburgh, but where it come from to Pittsburgh, I don't know. Maybe they stole it from the rebels down there.

"They were coming up around what they called the safe route because it was away from the southern troops in southern Pennsylvania, and they were headed east to have it minted at the Philadelphia mint. The only safe route was the northern one from Pittsburgh up through the Alleghenies and back down the Susquehanna, but a bunch of bandits or roughnecks, or whatever you want to call them, found out about it.

"The army force bivouacked at Saint Marys, and they left there, coming over here to Driftwood, where they could float it down the Susquehanna by boat. But somewhere between Driftwood and Saint Marys, they were attacked by these ruffians or outlaws, who killed them and made off with the gold.

"One team of mules and one Army sergeant, a Negro, ended up in Driftwood, where the Army came and got him. They questioned him, but he could never remember what happened, as far as anybody knew, and he eventually died in service. I know the Army has been hunting that shipment of gold ever since.

"But according to that old Army sergeant, the gold had been buried when they found out they were gonna be attacked. Then they took the horse and the mules and the wagon that was carrying the gold and they hid it. So, the gold has never turned up in the records anyplace, and Uncle Sam is still hunting it.

"Years ago, they used to send in a team every two or three years to try to figure it out, and I imagine they still got a record because it was Army gold, and the Army never forgets anything! National Geographic was in here once, and they were gonna run an article on it, but they never did because I think once they got in touch with Army command, it was squashed.

"I've heard that story ever since I was a kid growing up in Emporium, and it's over there at the bar. The whole damned story's printed out on a newspaper that was printed in Clearfield back at that time. And then, in Driftwood, behind the old bar across from the railroad station, the whole thing was there.

"I heard about it since I was big enough to walk because Dad was an engineer on the railroad. We lived in Emporium, and when I was growing up, there was all kinds of stories about people hunting for gold up on the mountain!"[3]

Some still search for that lost gold shipment, not only because of the amount of money involved but also because there is little doubt that the incident actually happened. Despite the fact the famous sharp-shooting "Bucktail" Regiment, so called because of the buck deer tails they wore in their caps, came from this area during the Civil War, there were still many Copperheads in these same counties at the time the gold shipment was ambushed.

These southern sympathizers would probably have been only too happy to steal some northern gold, especially if it would have enriched the coffers of the Confederacy and lined their own pockets. So, if the gold shipment

3. Howard Heggenstaller (born 1920), recorded November 16, 1989.

of 1863 was ambushed, as the legend states, then it may very well have been a robbery committed by a band of these Confederate allies.

Besides the fact that there were people in the area who may have had a motive for committing the gold shipment robbery, there was also an obvious path over which the gold may have been transported. Long before the turbulent times of the 1860s, there was another road through this same section dating back to the 1750s, the time of the French and Indian War.

This older military road, "much used by early settlers,"[4] ran from present-day Lock Haven through Renovo, Driftwood, and Emporium and then on to the Allegheny River. The route generally corresponds to the same route said to have been taken by the Army contingent escorting the wagon of gold during the Civil War, and despite the legendary claims that the gold has never been found, some think otherwise.

Up in Emporium, there was once a lot of talk about the millionaire, an eccentric who had come to town with nothing but who somehow eventually came into enough money that he was able to build a large hotel in a spot that everyone regarded as one that guaranteed the business would fail. Situated back in the mountains, near a remote water tower that railroad trains stopped at to take on water, the hotel was a fish out of water since there was never anyone else around to patronize the place.

Popular opinion was that the eccentric innkeeper had money to burn if he could do something as absurd as he had done, and the only apparent way he could have gotten that kind of money, most people agreed, was to have found the lost gold shipment. Opinion didn't change much after the man died, for stories then surfaced claiming that the old boy had requested that some of his gold be buried with him in his grave.

Speculative at best, the story of the millionaire and his hotel does nothing to prove or disprove the tale about the lost gold shipment. There are, however, parts of the lost gold shipment legend that are similar to tales related in other parts of the state. Although these other accounts may merely be based on the same legendary elements which are embedded in the story of the lost gold shipment of Elk and Cameron Counties, their similarities, on the other hand, may be an indication that the incidents recounted in them are based on facts after all. And there are at least two

---

4. J. E. Henretta, *Kane and the Upper Allegheny*, 156.

other tales that have details similar to those recounted in the Elk County story.

The first of these accounts was once popular in the Allegheny Mountains around the small community of Snow Shoe in Centre County. Here, it was once believed that six barrels of gold were hidden away in the mountains, near a hotel called the Mountain House, in 1864.

The reason for the concealment, according to this tale, was that many bank directors were in a panic, afraid that Confederate troops had a good chance of taking over the entire state. And rather than let their gold fall into the rebels' hands, the banks in the southern parts of the state decided to ship their gold reserves to safer ground in northern Pennsylvania.

What is certain today is that the Mountain House was built in 1859 by the Bellefonte and Snow Shoe Railroad Company, the same corporation that laid out the village of Snow Shoe in 1858. John Essington, landlord of this remote wayside inn around the time of the Civil War, was one of several innkeepers who eventually helped establish the lodge's reputation as the premier hotel of the town. However, despite the fact that the inn was once a well-frequented layover for travelers, the six barrels of gold purportedly buried nearby have never been found.

Another similar story of lost Civil War gold has also remained a popular Adams County tale since the time of the great conflict between the North and the South. Scars of that great struggle have not faded away entirely over the years, nor have the stories that grew out of it, and one of the ugliest scars left upon the region was the burning of the town of Chambersburg by Confederate forces in 1864.

"I know the Confederate army robbed Chambersburg and burnt it," recalled the old farmer from the South Mountains. "The reason they burnt it wasn't just for pure hate. They done it because the north burnt one of their towns. That's a true story; they got even. Well, they were shipping the gold east from out of Chambersburg, and they hid it in the mountains somewhere when they found out the Confederates entered the town. Then, later, those who hid the gold got killed before they could tell anyone where they hid it.

"Well, I have an idea where it is. It's east of Caledonia, between Cashtown and Fayetteville, and along the old National Pike coming through there. It's all growed up in trees now, and the road's been changed some, but that was an important highway that's been there a long time. But anyhow, they hid the gold and never came back, so I believe it's there. I think it's there, really!"[5]

The burning of the Franklin County town of Chambersburg by the Confederate forces of McCausland and Johnston on July 30, 1864, was one of the low points of the Civil War for residents of southern Pennsylvania. Undaunted by their defeat at Gettysburg the year before, the Rebel army under General Jubal Early had orders to burn the town of Chambersburg if the residents of the town refused to pay a ransom of $100,000 in gold. Unable to come up with that kind of money, the town's residents had to stand by and watch in disbelief as their homes went up in flames.

Firsthand accounts of the episode describe the way citizens of the town were stopped on the street by Confederate soldiers and robbed of all their valuables. The relief of those citizens who were fortunate enough to avoid being robbed on the streets was often short-lived. Other accounts of the raid tell of how the Rebels plundered homes of silverware, jewels, clothes, and anything else of value, oftentimes putting the house to the torch after stripping away the wealth within.

The citizens of Chambersburg were not exactly strangers to the visits of an invasion force. During the fall of 1862, Jeb Stuart's cavalry also raided the town, and in the summer of 1863, General Robert E. Lee's troops, on their way to a meeting with destiny at a peaceful country town called Gettysburg, had swept through the area, robbing Chambersburg's farmers of wagons, horses, and grain.

It was only natural, given the experiences of invasions by Confederate forces on two other occasions, that with a threat of yet a third invasion in 1864, the people of Franklin County would take whatever measures they could to avoid losing their valuables. A contingency plan seemed especially necessary to them since no Union troops appeared to be forthcoming to do battle with the Rebels. With the notice that Jubal Early's troops had crossed the Potomac, the farmers and merchants of Chambersburg began to remove their livestock and other things they valued, and residents of the town knew that their actions were sound ones.

---

5. Jim Stephens (born 1924), recorded December 23, 1989.

"That farmers should send away their horses and merchants their goods, at the approach of the enemy, is not only natural but eminently wise and proper," noted one citizen who experienced the raid firsthand. "Allowing them to remain at home," he reasoned, "without the ability to defend them from capture, would be giving aid and comfort to the enemy."[6]

The mass withdrawal of personal valuables that occurred in Franklin County prior to the invasion of 1864 makes it more probable that banks there would have followed suit, removing their money and gold as well. This is undoubtedly just what happened, and such actions are similar to what could have prompted the shipments of gold referred to in the legends of Elk and Centre Counties.

The question remains, however, whether any of the treasures mentioned in these old legends were ever found. If not, then some lucky person may yet find them someday, and it would not be the first time someone got rich by finding one of Pennsylvania's lost treasures, like the two Montour County men who got lucky one cold November day in 1884.

Details of their windfall appeared in the November 27, 1884, edition of the *Berwick Independent*, and the account may offer some encouragement for today's treasure hunters:

One Saturday afternoon of last week, while Frank Lewis and Jack Gearhart were digging fern roots on the island three miles below Danville, they unearthed an iron box that was completely covered with rust. To their utter astonishment, they found it filled with gold and silver coins of a very ancient date. Mr. Kinter (a railway agent), being an expert, took charge of the counting, and after 10 hours of steady work he had the money counted out in $1,000.00 piles amounting to $47,000. Mr. Kinter assures Messrs. Gearhart and Lewis that by strictly adhering to their usual temperate habits, they can lay by the shovel and hoe for the rest of their lives and live in ease and comfort.

The general supposition is that the money was placed there by Captain Kidd sometime in the 16th century. Being hard-pressed on the Chesapeake Bay by other pirates, he entered the Susquehanna River and sailed

---

6. Reverend B. S. Schneck, *The Burning of Chambersburg, Pennsylvania*, 33.

up Crook's Riffles, which at the time formed part of the island. In order to save the money, he buried it.[7]

Perhaps there will be others who will one day be as lucky as Mr. Lewis and Mr. Gearhart. It's hard to imagine the excitement that accompanied the discovery of the box of coins in 1884, but the interest generated then would pale in comparison to the stir the event would create now. Today, such a discovery would receive comprehensive media attention of all sorts, prompting a whole host of treasure hunters to dust off their metal detectors and head for the hills to seek out the lost gold and silver fortunes still hidden away in Pennsylvania's romance-filled mountains.

EPILOGUE: The quest for the army gold in Elk or Cameron Counties has continued to this day. Over the years, it became known as the Dent's Run treasure, and as it seems, my Potter County informant was correct when he noted that "the army never forgets." The Federal government had been to the area several times in the past, but they sent the FBI back again in March of 2018 to conduct a major excavation in Elk State Forest Land near the small Elk County town of Dent's Run.

This time, it appeared that they meant business, bringing backhoes, bulldozers, and other heavy equipment to the dig site and stationing armed guards wearing bullet-proof vests to secure the area. Two local men, who had led the Federals to the spot where the men had been credited with having found evidence of the buried gold in the first place, were not allowed to the site at all. Then, after all was said and done, the FBI claimed they had found nothing.

The two original local finders were not convinced, and to this day, they feel that the FBI, for whatever reason, does not want to reveal that they had found the gold bars and had carted them away on that cold March night in 2018. The two treasure hunters say they've used their metal detectors to rescan the area after the government's excavations, the same detectors they used to detect the gold at this same spot, and they have now detected no gold there at all.

---

7. Author unknown, "Lost Treasure Tales Include Danville," news article appearing in *The Daily Item* of Danville, Pennsylvania, unknown date.

It's this evidence and doubts as to government claims about the FBI excavations that make treasure hunters wonder if the Dent's Run gold stash is yet to be discovered after all![8]

NOTE: One of the boys of Colonel Thomas Kane's Bucktail Regiment found a way to mine some gold in his unique way. According to a history of that noted Civil War unit, Colonel Thomas Kane conceived the idea for his regiment's name when he first saw bucktails dangling from the caps of his recruits. The decorations on the Bucktail soldiers' hats were also admired by their fellow Union soldiers to the point where they wanted their own. The demand was insistent enough that one industrious Potter County boy wrote home for a supply of bucktails, "which he sold to his buddies for a quarter apiece!"[9]

8. Cullen Murphy, "A Mad Hunt for Civil War Treasure," *The Atlantic*, July/August 2022.
9. Mary E. Welfling, "Bucktail Regiment Famous in Civil War," *Historical Sketches of Potter County*, 238.

CHAPTER 10

CAMPBELL'S LEDGE

Throughout the entire Wyoming Valley of Luzerne County there are few landmarks more prominent than Campbell's Ledge. Towering over the North Branch of the Susquehanna River and opposite the town of Exeter along Route 92, this imposing rock face rises to a height of 1,364 feet above sea level and almost 600 feet above the valley below. The size and age of such an enormous cliff are enough to make it historically noteworthy in its own right, and much has been written about the place over the years. However, there still seems to be a bit of uncertainty about how the cliff got its name, with history and legend each preserving different versions of the origins of the ledge's title. Nonetheless, in this case, it would appear that legend, rather than history, supplies us with the true story.

Early historical records of the Wyoming Valley do contain many graphic details of the numerous Indian raids that were inflicted upon the settlers of that area during the Revolutionary War. It was during one of these bloody episodes, so says the old legend about Campbell's Ledge, that an event so remarkable occurred that it prompted the survivors to rename the prominent geological landmark along present-day Route 92. On the other hand, many scholars have claimed that there are no hard facts in the historical record that uphold the legendary explanation, and so academics have dismissed the legend in favor of their own conclusions.

As it sometimes happens in these matters, once the experts give a popular historical explanation a blessing, it becomes hard to displace, especially when there is no historical evidence to support alternate ideas, especially

A view of Campbell's Ledge. As it looks towering over Coxton Road near Duryea in Luzerne County - taken by the author during a rainy day in December of 2023.

those of the legendary kind. With this thought in mind, it's easy to see why historians willingly accepted the conclusions of their predecessors when it came to the history behind the name of the famous ledge in the Wyoming Valley.

However, unmindful of the hard, cold facts, the old legend refuses to die. It's still a popular tale, told and retold by the descendants of those who settled the valley during those times when Native Americans took up the hatchet and swept down upon unsuspecting settlements.

Accounts of that period tell of blazing cabins filling the skies with dense clouds of smoke and of the blood of massacred settlers coloring the soil red. And it is those same lurid pen pictures that have colored the legendary tale of Campbell's Ledge.

Despite their differences of opinion, history and legend do agree on one thing, and that is that the Wyoming Valley's Indian troubles served as the basis for the naming of Campbell's Ledge. However, the two diverge quite remarkably at that point, with history claiming that the name of the

View From Campbell's Ledge. Looking out over the Susquehanna River and the town of West Pittston from the edge of 1,280 foot high Campbell's Ledge. This is the place where legend says early pioneer Campbell rode off on his horse to escape a band of pursuing Indians. (Photo courtesy of Dave Miller - MyHikes.org.)

ledge can be traced back to the pen of a peaceful poet and legend stating that the landmark's title is rooted in those days of Indian warfare when the scalping knife and fire brand were the scourge of the Wyoming Valley.

Out of all the terrible incidents that occurred in that valley during the Revolutionary War, probably the most infamous was the massacre that took place almost two years to the day after the signing of the Declaration of Independence. It was on the third day of July, Independence month, 1778, that the infamous Wyoming Massacre took place, resulting in a widespread exodus of settlers throughout the Pennsylvania frontier, a panic that would later be remembered as The Great Runaway. But it was the horrible slaughter at Wyoming that stood out among all the other bloody incidents that occurred at this time and, according to one historian, "shocked the world and brought deep sympathy for the American cause."[1]

The historian's statement was a true one, for news of the incident at Wyoming spread rapidly throughout the American colonies, and even traveled across the sea, where it struck a particularly sensitive chord with a Scottish poet named Thomas Campbell. Campbell was so moved by the stories of the sufferings of those who were victims of the Indian's wrath at Wyoming that they inspired him to compose a poem that captured the scenes of the event in words that only a poet can produce.

Those words in his "Gertrude of Wyoming" struck a chord with others as well, and the poem became a famous rhyme—so famous, in fact, that his heroine Gertrude would become as closely identified with Wyoming as the poet Longfellow's heroine Evangeline became associated with Acadia.

Aware of peoples' tendency to associate Thomas Campbell with the story of the Wyoming Massacre, historians took that association a step further and assumed that Campbell's Ledge was named after the same poet as well. However, this is an incorrect assumption, at least according to the legend, which claims it was an unrecorded historical event that is the basis for the name of the prominent cliff.

"You could see it from where we lived. You could see this ledge, you know, in the distance from where we lived," recalled the native son of the Wyoming Valley who had heard the area's legends from the time he was old enough to understand.

"There was this story about Campbell," continued the former Pittston resident who had heard the story from his parents when he was just a young lad. "Campbell was in charge of a militia unit or something at the time of the French and Indian War, and he was scouting all along the top of that mountain. Well, the Indians were camped there, and whether they came across him or whether he discovered one of their camps, they started chasing him and were gonna kill him. They had horses, but he outran them

---

1. Paul A. W. Wallace, *Indians in Pennsylvania*, 160.

on his horse until he realized that the only chance he had was to get into the river.

"Well, at that time, the river was really high, and it ran under the ledge; it's pretty far from there now, you know. But he leaped off the ledge on his horse, and his horse broke its neck when it hit the water. It was a pretty high jump, and his horse got killed, but he survived. Well, he was in the river then, and he was okay because there was no way they could catch him since at the time, the Susquehanna River had a hell of a current. He just escaped along the river and got back to the settlement and warned them that the Indians were in that area. I never heard anything about him after that, but that's how Campbell's Ledge got its name."[2]

Perhaps one of the reasons that historians prefer to ignore this old legendary account that claims to be the basis for the naming of Campbell's Ledge is because the story does indeed have legendary qualities. Typical of any legend, the tale of Indian scout Campbell's fantastic escape from certain death is not all that unique, apparently tending to travel from one place to another. However, unlike other legends that often have to migrate thousands of miles before they find a second home, this story lazily settled on a red sandstone ledge of eight hundred feet in height located only about eighteen miles south of Campbell's Ledge.

This other impressive cliff is today known as Tilbury Knob, but it was formerly called Rampart Rocks because of a battle of that name which was fought there during the struggle between Connecticut and Pennsylvania settlers for control of the region during the last quarter of the eighteenth century. The quaint legend of how Rampart Rocks got a new name was passed on to me by another lover of the old-time tales; a migrant himself, he was living in Philipsburg, Pennsylvania, when I interviewed him. According to the old gentleman's legendary account, Tilbury Knob was named for an early settler named Tilbury, who, in the early 1700s, rode his horse over the ledge to escape Indians.

"Knowing the way Indians drove buffalo over cliffs out west, they probably thought it was a good place to trap a white man," claimed the former Wilkes-Barre resident, who concluded his narrative by stating that

---

2. Ken Davis (born 1905), interviewed February 2, 1974.

"Tilbury's horse was impaled on a tree, which saved his life. He was able to crawl down out of the tree and then swim safely to Nanticoke."[3]

Although the historical record of the many Indian battles in the Wyoming Valley would agree that incidents like those preserved in the Tilbury Knob or Campbell's Ledge legends could have been based on real events, it seems like too much of a stretch to believe that two very similar fantastic escapes such as these could have happened so close geographically. One account just may be a distorted version of the other, localized to a different section.

However, the doubt remains as to which account, if one is indeed based on fact, is the true one. It's a question that can't be answered with any certainty today, but it's interesting to note that there are indeed other places in the state that are also said to be named after similarly remarkable but unverifiable events.

Although it's a bit of a digression, there's another account from the Wyoming Valley that shows just how difficult it often is to put any stamp of authenticity on a legend. This episode also involves another Wyoming Valley landmark, a small hillock located directly across from Tilbury Knob and known locally as Honeypot Knob.

The unusual name comes from the fact that on the knob's peak is a bowl-like depression in which honeysuckle vines grow profusely during the summer months. Although a place of natural beauty, it was here, according to local legend, that the so-called Grasshopper War took place one summer day. However, no historical records mention such a battle and details about it are preserved only in legendary accounts, which agree in most respects except for where the struggle actually occurred.

According to the Wyoming Valley version of the legend, one summer day, some Shawnee Indian women and their children were peacefully gathering fruit from bushes and trees, which grew at the foot of a small elevation the early settlers would later call Honeypot Knob. Not too far away a group of Delaware Indian women and their children were picking fruit as well.

Usually, such a scene would have been a pleasant one: warm summer breezes filling the air with the fragrance of honeysuckle flowers, dusky

3. W. G. Jones (born 1905), interviewed February 2, 1974.

Indian maidens busily picking berries from blackberry or huckleberry bushes, and laughing Indian children finding delight in even the simplest of nature's creations.

All seemed content and peaceful until one of the children found a large grasshopper and began playing with it. The insect attracted the attention of a child from the other tribe who wanted to play with it, too. But the finder of the bug was not willing to share it, and a squabble broke out.

Soon, the mothers were involved, and an argument started over which group had territorial rights to this particular area. Then, more children and women joined the fight until they were all in the fray. At this point the warriors returned from a peaceful hunting trip, and they immediately jumped into the melee to protect their families.

The contest turned out to be a long and bloody affair, and, according to the legend, when the sun finally sank behind the hills, the last rays of sunlight fell upon a battlefield strewn with corpses, which were mostly those of the Shawnee's finest warriors. It was as a result of this victory, claims the legend, that the Delawares were able to expel the Shawnees from the valley.[4]

As intriguing as this story is, it seems to have the same problem as the Tilbury Knob story in that it can't quite decide where it should call home. Up in the center of the state, for example, there is an identical legend that claims that the Grasshopper War took place along the banks of Licking Creek in Juniata County and that the combatants were Delawares and Tuscaroras. But regardless of which county has a legitimate claim to the Grasshopper War, the story appears to be a curious example of a legend being relocated to a different spot from where it may have actually happened.

After a re-location such as this, it is difficult, if not impossible, to determine where the original event may have occurred. This, in turn, casts doubt on the certainty of whether or not the event even happened at all—it may have just been a tall tale of that day and age. However, in the Juniata County case, there is a monument that backs up their claims, and the Book Indian Mound, as it's called locally, is supposedly the mass burial place of the warriors killed in that contest.

4. Sherman Day, *Historical Collections of Pennsylvania*, 432.

It's unusual to have tangible evidence like this that confirms a legend's legitimacy, and so in most cases, all that can be done is to look at the historical facts in order to determine whether events recalled by the legend could have possibly happened, and this is exactly how we'll look at the legend of Campbell's Ledge.

Anyone who reads the history of the Wyoming Valley will find that over 275 years ago, around 1737, Campbell's Ledge overlooked the site of an Indian village known as Assarughney. It was probably not a place where a European settler would have wanted to tarry very long since many residents of the settlement were Delaware Indians who had been forced off their homelands and pushed to the west as a result of being cheated by the infamous Walking Purchase.

This deceitful scheme by the heirs of William Penn alienated the Delaware against Pennsylvania more than any other misdeed. It was, they said, a deciding factor in their decision to take up arms against Pennsylvania during the French and Indian War that would flare up twenty years later.

In addition to providing a home base for the many Delaware Indians who lived here and who most probably harbored an intense dislike of European settlers in general, Assarughney was sometimes a layover for itinerant Indian warriors, who would most likely not have been all that friendly either. Many were probably in raiding parties traveling along the Great Warriors Path, the famous Indian trail that came down from Tioga in the north to Shamokin and points south, passing directly beneath Campbell's Ledge along the way. And warriors in war parties like these would have been in a belligerent mood, psyching themselves up to do battle with their enemy tribes in the Carolinas.

The prominent ledge probably evoked strong emotions in the Indians when they saw it, perhaps because it would have been a reminder of their many wars with their enemies. This would have made it a special place for them, and it apparently was not just an ordinary landmark to the early settlers either.

Early historical accounts say they used it practically and referred to it as Dial Rock. The reason for the odd name was because the stone face near the summit is always in shadow, but at precisely midday, the rays of the sun

View of the Book Indian Mound, as it looked in May of 2010. Located near Academia in Beale Township, Juniata County, this site is listed on the National Register of Historic Places and marks the site where, in 1929, 26 Indian skeletons were found interred. At one time it was 15 feet high and covered an eighth of an acre. However, in 1929 it was practically nonexistent due to digging by relic hunters and curiosity seekers. Back in 1886 locals believed that the mound was a burial site for warriors that were killed in a battle between warring Indian tribes.

fall on the shadowy face of the ledge, signaling the noon hour just as clearly as the hands on a clock.

Even if the Indians didn't view the ledge in any special way, they certainly did not consider the Wyoming Valley as merely another place to live, and they fought the colonists harder for no land than they fought for this place. The whole area was one that the Shawanese, Nanticokes, and Delaware Indians must have thought of as their paradise. Game of all sorts was particularly abundant in this unspoiled Eden, and the stream and river contained plenty of fish like trout and shad.

Crops of corn and squash also grew well here, as did wild grapes and wild berries of all types. In fact, it might be said that conditions here were as close as an Indian could get to his Happy Hunting Ground without actually dying and going on to the next world. If so, then it is of little wonder that when settlers men began to move into the Wyoming Valley, it became the scene of many bloody Indian battles and massacres.

The first massacre that occurred in the Wyoming Valley took place in October of 1763 when 135 Delaware Indians killed about 20 settlers who were at work in their fields, a slaughter that signaled the opening of what was to become a campaign of terror.

Thinking that the Six Nations had promised them the Wyoming lands as their permanent hunting grounds and place of abode, the Delaware learned that the great Iroquois Confederacy had sold the land out from under them, and they meant to exact their revenge. Other major massacres followed in 1778, 1779, and 1780, but numerous others occurred throughout the valley at times between 1763 and 1778. During the years 1772 and 1773, in particular, there was a widespread fear of attack, and the people lived in forts.

Such conditions are the stuff of which tall tales and legends are made, but they also can be the setting for actual events that take on legendary proportions, and it is in this gray area in which the legend of Campbell's Ledge seems to fall. It may just be a tall tale, but it has enough of a historical ring to it that at least one of the earliest Wyoming Valley historians included the account in his history of the valley.

"There is a wild legend which has given the name to this ledge," states George Peck in his interesting history. "The Indians pursued a man named

A closer view of the Book Indian Mound. This is the monument marking the hallowed ground, which is largely concealed by a shady copse of trees. Not even the wind stirred their branches when we stood quietly here in May of 2010 and contemplated what might have happened at this spot sometime in the dim past.

Campbell. He had taken refuge in the ravines of this mountain, where there are many fine living springs and where thick foliage afforded a safe shelter. But the fierce Red Men are on his track. He is on old enemy and is singled out for special torture.

"He knows his fate if taken. He tries every path that winds out into the deeper forest but without success. He is hemmed in like the roe by the relentless wolves. But he does not hesitate; he springs forward to the verge of the hanging rock. One glance behind him shows him that escape is utterly hopeless. The shouts of the savages are heard as they rush upon their prey. With a scream of defiance, he leaps into the friendly arms of death."[5]

One final fact should be mentioned that may interest those who enjoy discovering the odd and old events of times gone by—a fact that indirectly supports the theory that Campbell's Ledge was named from a singular

5. George Peck, D.D., *Wyoming—History, Stirring Incidents, and Romantic Adventures,* 348.

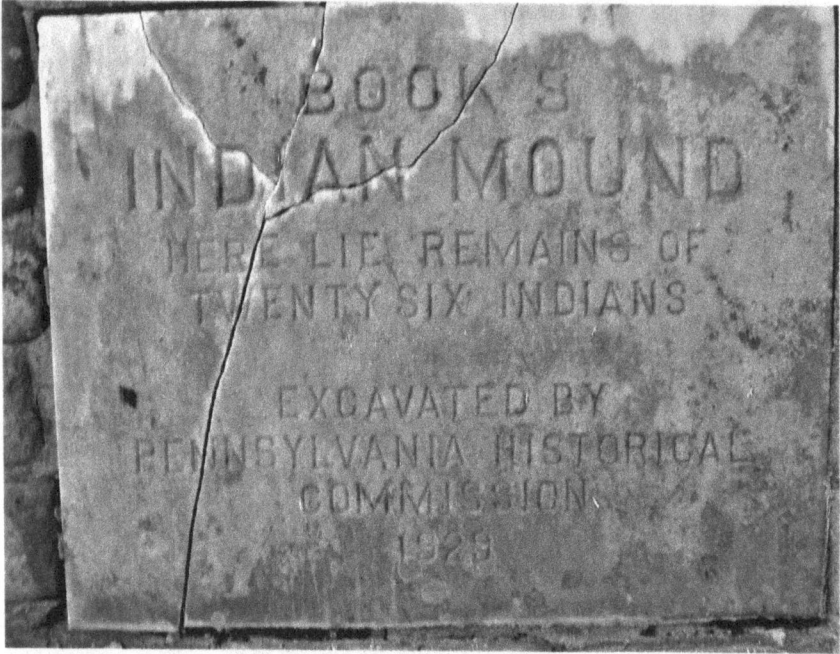

Inscripton on the Book Indian Mound. The engraving reads: "Book's Indian Mound. Here lie the remains of twenty-six Indians. Excavated by the Pennsylvania Historical Commission 1929."

event that occurred there. The historical records from those days of Indian warfare prove that there were many fearless and notable men of that period, but there were some whose courage and deeds of valor were so outstanding that they were awarded a special degree of respect. One such man was Samuel Brady, an Indian fighter and frontier scout from Lycoming County.

An early biographer of Sam Brady states that Brady's very name was enough to quiet the fears of settlers' children when they were assured that Captain Brady and his rangers were on watch. The Indians indeed regarded Sam Brady as one of their greatest enemies and a man they wanted to capture and torture in the most horrible ways they could devise. And there was one time when they actually captured him but missed their chance to see him die in their hands.

On this one occasion, Brady and a party of his rangers had followed a party of Indian scalp hunters into the Indian country of Ohio. He and his men were all captured and firmly bound as the Indians prepared their special torments, feeling sure that he would be able to endure more pain than any captive they had ever tortured. However, at the last possible moment, Brady was able to break away.

He, too, was pursued by warriors, and in order to escape, he had to make a fantastic leap of twenty-five feet or more across a chasm between two bluffs. The Indians, believing no man could jump like this, concluded that Brady was a wild turkey and had flown across. They then carved a picture of a wild turkey's foot onto the rock where their foe had landed. To this day, the spot is known as Brady's Hill.

There is also a Brady's Creek in Allegheny County, named after the same man, and other such locations that took their names from other early idols of the times could also be mentioned. But the point is that during those times, landmarks were often named after exceptional individuals whose larger-than-life deeds at those spots were particularly significant to the early settlers of that area. Campbell's Ledge may be another such place, but in this case, the legend, if true, raises only doubts and leaves us with a shadowy figure who would have been considered a hero of that day and age.

NOTE: There is yet another historical account that confuses the issue as to whether Campbell's Ledge legend is based on a true event or just another popular folk myth. In an 1857 deposition in Meginness's *Otzinachson,* an elderly resident of Muncy, Mr. Jacob Cook of Lycoming County, claimed that when he was younger, he recalled older citizens of that area telling of an event very similar to that which supposedly happened at Campbell's Ledge. In Mr. Cook's own words,

"About the time of the Indian troubles, a man named Marcus Huling, living in the town of Northumberland, was on the west side of the river when a number of Indians chased him. He ran as swiftly as he could toward the precipice at Blue Hill, but they gained so rapidly upon him that he expected to be taken there. They also fancied him secure in their grasp. Being drove to the edge of the frightful precipice, with the savages yelling in his ear, he determined to make the dreadful leap, preferring to die in this manner rather than fall beneath the tomahawk of the Indian.

"Seizing a large branch of a tree in his hands, he jumped over and landed some ninety feet below, on a shelf of rock, unhurt! From this point, he jumped forty feet further and escaped with only the dislocation of his shoulder. The savages were obliged to run round for a mile when he escaped. This jump, if true, is certainly the greatest one on record. It is supposed the branch broke his fall and saved his life. Huling, upon being asked about it, replied that he 'jumped for a great wager—he jumped to save his life!'"[6]

---

6. J. F. Meginness, *Otzinachson*, 621.

CHAPTER 11

CAST INTO STONE

Sometime in the years ahead, there may be a reader of these lines who will want to try to collect the old-time legends and folktales similar to the ones recorded in the present volume and the other volumes of this series. Although the individual may have some luck in their endeavors, they will find that time is the enemy of such a commendable task; the rate at which these relics of a bygone age are disappearing increases with the passing of each year.

Tellers of the old episodes are now "up in their seventies" or older, and the younger generations seem less inclined to pass the accounts on to their children. Nonetheless, it does seem likely that there will always be sanctuaries for the narratives somewhere in our mountains—places where the tales have already survived for so long, not only because they are interesting but also because the people there seem to appreciate them more. If that is true, then one of these sanctuaries will be the hills and valleys of southern Pennsylvania.

Every year, thousands of tourists drive through the south-central part of our state on their way to see the National Military Park at Gettysburg, and it's probably safe to say that almost none of them realize that they are driving through that section of ridges Pennsylvanians call the South Mountains. Almost everyone has heard of the Blue Ridge Mountains of Virginia and North Carolina, that rugged stretch of Appalachia where tales of moonshiners, hardy mountaineers, and unsurpassed mountain vistas await the visitor. But Pennsylvania's South Mountains, even though they are the northernmost extension of the Blue Ridge chain, are not as widely heralded as their southern cousins.

Nonetheless these Pennsylvania hills abound with the same kind of legendary lore. Consequently, it's probably fair to say that the South Mountains still rank among the most legend-shrouded peaks in the entire state. Tales of ghosts, witches, and Indians can still be heard here today in the Cumberland Valley, told just as they were a hundred years ago. Nonetheless, although many such stories are awaiting the collector, none can probably tweak the imagination more than the legend of the Indian sentry of the South Mountains.

Down in Franklin County there is a prominent elevation among the South Mountains that was known locally at one time as Caledonia Mountain. The small ridge that looms over Thaddeus Stevens' old iron furnace is known today as Rocky Mountain, which is more in keeping with the condition of the surface of the land on the mountaintop.

Located in Michaux State Forest, Rocky Mountain frowns down upon Caledonia State Park and also upon the site of the old Graffenburg Inn, that ancient hostelry that was once a favorite stopping place for travelers passing through the South Mountains. Destroyed by fire some twenty or thirty years ago, the Graffenburg Inn is now only a name found in the history books, a fate that at least guarantees the old hostelry some measure of immortality. Unfortunately, the same cannot be said for the Indian warrior whose stone face on top of Rocky Mountain gazes stoically out over the Cumberland Valley.

Many hikers have undoubtedly walked past the silent sentinel numerous times. The Appalachian Trail lies right next to the unusual stone formation, but probably very few passersby have ever even noticed a face on the rocks. Surprisingly, there are supposed to be two such profiles on the mountain; one the result of glacial action or some other natural weathering process, and the other sculpted by the hand of man. The face formed naturally is the one associated with the curious legend that is said to have come down to us from the Indians who once lived here, while this natural likeness no doubt prompted someone, perhaps an old stone mason, to sculpt the other face into the rock.

Photo of Sentinel Rock in 1900. The photo of this natural wonder was published in an article in the Gettysburg Compiler *of Gettysburg in 1900. Arguably one of the most amazing natural likenesses of a human profile anyone has ever seen, it clearly showed the humanlike features of hair, eyes, nose, mouth, forehead, chin, and neck. Copy is blurry since it was newsprint.*

The Sentinel Rock pillar. We searched for years to find Sentinel Rock, not believing that this was really it, despite being directed here by park rangers. Then a local hiker and lover of local history showed us that it really is the real thing—the real Sentinel Rock after all. (Photo courtesy of Len Kapp.)

One reason hikers miss the faces may be that there are more obvious attractions for those who make the steep trek up the mountain. Fine views of eastern Franklin County and western Adams County can be enjoyed from the trail, and near here are some lofty rock ledges known as Buzzards Peak, where buzzards can be seen on occasion. Why the buzzards picked this particular spot to frequent is not exactly clear, but perhaps they were drawn here in the same manner they were attracted to the number of dead lying on the battlefield after the battle at Gettysburg.

It seems that once buzzards are drawn to a choice spot, they tend to stay there, as do their offspring, and it's said that that is why there are so many buzzards to be seen even today at the Gettysburg battlefield. Others say that the buzzards were always there and that the battle had nothing to do with attracting them from somewhere else.

However, if the explanation for the presence of so many buzzards at Gettysburg is true, then the explanation for the buzzards that make their home on Caledonia Mountain could lie in the legend about this place if the story has any basis in fact. On the other hand, the buzzards do seem to get scarcer every year, just like the number of people who know about Caledonia Mountain's Indian face and the legend behind it that reads like a Greek tragedy.

Probably the main reason that hikers never see the stone face is that they never look for it. Very few people know about the legend today, and that's probably because it's so old, its origins rooted in the misty annals of the mountains prior to the time when any settlers had even entered this area. The legend, which still surfaces from time to time in some villages and valleys of Franklin County, recalls the time when the Munsees, a branch of the Delaware Indians that was also known as the Wolf Tribe, could be found in the forest around Caledonia.

The Munsees and the powerful Iroquois Confederacy known as the Six Nations were, during this period, reaching the end of what had been years of struggle over control of native lands throughout various parts of the state. This seemingly endless warfare had taken its toll upon the Munsees, so much so that their numbers and the lands they controlled were dwindling.

Eventually, so states the legend, the tiny band of Delawares was pushed westward until one day they found themselves in a small valley to the west of the ridge we now call Rocky Mountain. Knowing that their Iroquois enemies were following them, the Munsees took extra precautions to ensure the safety of their families.

Every night, they would post a lookout on the mountain in whose shadow they were encamped. The sentry was instructed, in the words of one early account, to "shoot an arrow, marked by a knot of buckskin, into the lodge of his brethren if he saw the hated warriors of the Six Nations approach by day, and to set fire with his flints the piles of brush if he should discover them coming by night."[1]

"One night, the camp went to sleep, and as the sentry was doing the watch, an Indian maiden, who was a daughter of one of the tribe's warriors, come out and said she'd set with him," claimed a South Mountains farmer who recalled the rest of the narrative for me one day when we were driving out to Caledonia to see if we could find the interesting face on the mountain.

"He told her it's not a woman's place to be with a warrior when he's guarding," continued the old gentleman. "So she said, 'Never mind. There'll be two of us to watch and hear.'

"And she still protested, but she insisted in the ways of a woman, and, you know, they'll get their way! So, she stayed with him. Well, they fell asleep together instead of listening and watching, and the Iroquois came into the camp that night and wiped out everybody except this girl's father and the shamus or witch doctor. So, the only ones that were left were those two, but actually, the tribe was literally wiped out there."[2]

Another source for the legend described the attack in more romanticized terms, noting that the arrows of the Iroquois fell "like hail from an overcast sky" and that the invaders "buried their tomahawks and battle axes in men, women, and children until the lodge was quiet as before—only that the sleep of the braves was deeper now than then."[3]

Despite some differences in details, all accounts agree on what happened next, and that was that the girl's father and the shamus realized that the sentry had probably not done his duty, and they went looking for him. He had been mortally wounded, and so was near death when they found him on the mountaintop. Next to him lay the lifeless body of the young maiden, her head split open by a tomahawk.

"Her father was very sad about his daughter being killed, but he didn't have any animosity toward the warrior boy who should have been watching

1. "Ancient Legend About Indian Sentry on Caledonia Mountain," article appeared in *The Gettysburg Times* on December 27, 1975; but was reprinted from an article which originally appeared in *The Gettysburg Compiler* on August 21, 1900.

2. Jim Stephens (born 1924), recorded December 23, 1989.

3. C. Hale Sipe, *The Indian Wars of Pennsylvania*, 743.

The Indian Sentinel. A close-up view of the Indian face. Viewed from the correct angle it becomes more apparent that the Gettysburg Compiler photo was taken here. However, over a century of weathering and freeze / thaw cycles have taken their toll, and the likeness is fast disappearing, perhaps freeing the soul of the negligent Indian sentinel at last! (Photo courtesy of Len Kapp.)

the trail," continued the old farmer as he tried to remember the story as best as he could.

"But the shamus, he was extremely angry, and he cast the boy's spirit into those rocks. And henceforth and forevermore, he shall watch the pass, and he shall never rest. His eyes shall be open, but he won't be able to see, and his ears will be there, but he won't be able to hear, and he shall always watch the pass."[4]

Today, the old legend of the sentry of the South Mountains seems like a fairy tale, but there are historical truths embedded in the ancient account, and a pursuit of those truths reveals some interesting possibilities as far as what the origin of the story might have been. The search for the facts behind the legend begins in the times before the Europeans came to America.

For centuries prior to European colonization, there had been a history of intertribal warfare between the numerous Indian tribes of Pennsylvania. There was no continual warfare, but it occurred frequently enough that the times of peace were appreciated and enjoyed. Mary Jemison, known as The White Woman of the Genesee, was captured by Indians when she was a child in Pennsylvania (see the author's Volume 7 for more details about Mary Jemison's capture and life and the recent discovery of the Jemison homestead site in Adams County).

She subsequently lived with the Indians of the Genesee Valley in New York State for seventy years, claiming that "No people can live more happily than that Indians did in times of peace; their lives were a continual round of pleasures. Their wants were few and easily satisfied, and their cares were only for today. If peace ever dwelt with men, it was in former times, in the recesses from war."[5]

Strategy was as much a part of Indian warfare as it is in modern-day battles, with the element of surprise being one of the primary objectives of any raiding party. "Surprise and stratagem are as often employed by them as open force,"[6] claimed one historian whose first-hand accounts of those times are among the best records of the Indian way of life in Pennsylvania.

"Courage, art, and circumspection are the essential and indispensable qualifications of an Indian warrior. When war is once begun, each one strives to excel in displaying them by stealing upon his enemy unawares, and deceiving and surprising him in various ways. On drawing near to

4. Jim Stephens (born 1924), recorded December 23, 1989.
5. C. Hale Sipe, *The Indian Wars of Pennsylvania*, 743.
6. Reverend John Heckewelder, *History of the Indian Nations*, 106, 177.

an enemy's country, they endeavor as much as possible to conceal their tracks."[7]

Evidence of some of those early Indian battles has been found at various places in the state. Large quantities of war relics, such as arrowheads and spearheads, as well as many skeletal remains found at Duncan's Island near Harrisburg, have led to the conclusion that a large battle was fought in that area. Similar sites have been found near Millerstown (Perry County), Tuscarora (Schuylkill County), and Standing Stone (Huntingdon County).

The South Mountains, too, certainly saw their share of battles between Indians and settlers during the French and Indian War when these hills were a kind of natural barrier between the settlers of Adams County and the Indians to the west. Even before that terrible struggle, the sound of the war-whoop or the sight of warriors painted for war was not uncommon here, for it was through this very section that the Virginia Path, or Great Trail, wound its way toward Maryland and the Carolinas.

The Great Trail was the easternmost Iroquois war path used by the Cherokees and Catawbas on their raids into Pennsylvania or by the Iroquois on their raids south. There were other warrior paths in Pennsylvania besides the Great Trail, all running north to south. Some of these, however, were not used by raiding parties but were called warrior paths by the early settlers anyway, merely because traders did not commonly use them. So, there were warrior paths in Huntingdon County, Greene County, and Clearfield County.

There was also the Great Warrior Path, which followed the Susquehanna River. Then there was the Virginia Path, and it is the one that came closest to the Indian face in the South Mountains. The approximate route of this true warrior path through southern Pennsylvania was from Harrisburg, through Carlisle, to Shippensburg, and then to Chambersburg and south, which means that the trail passed within ten miles of the stone face.

Perhaps the first South Mountain settlers or some of their descendants found the likeness on the rock, and knowing about the location of the Great Trail and also about the many Indian warriors who once frequented this area, created the legend. They would, no doubt, have heard something of the Tuscarora Indians (a branch of the Iroquois) who lived in Franklin

7. Ibid.

County at one time, and they might have known even a little about how the Indians conducted their raids.

Intriguing details like this may have proved inspiring enough to prompt some creative individuals to invent the story about the stone face. On the other hand, there is just as much reason to think that the legend could have come down to us from the Indian tribes that lived in this area. Details in the legend do agree with the Indians' descriptions of the way a raiding party conducted the business.

"A long time ago, my tribe was at war with our enemy of the south-land, the Cherokees, or *Oh-ya-dah*, the cave-dweller, and often called the People of the Red," recalled old Iroquois storyteller Jesse Cornplanter. "This happened when a war party was on its way to the land of the *Oh-ya-dah* to come back with as many scalps as it can. Now, it seems in those times they had a head chief in command in every war party. It was his duty to give thanks every morning as they got up before they ate their morning meal.

"It was the custom in those days to take their time in their march to the enemy country, to conserve their strength for the coming battle. So it took many days before they reached their destination. Every night, upon retiring, the head chief would cause warriors to stand guard at a certain distance and there to give alarm in case of attack."[8]

At this point, the Iroquois account departs from historical facts and enters a fantasy realm that many Indians once considered to be as real as the everyday world of sight and sound. In the land of Indian legends, strange things sometimes happened when a band of warriors was on the warpath—or at least to this one particular band, which had to seek shelter when a terrific storm blew in one night.

"As the storm heightened in intensity the band of warriors noticed what seemed like sparks of fire flying with the wind. All at once, they saw a monster head with its long hair whirling in all directions. Now, it seems this monster head was the power of this windstorm, as the trees of the forest just snapped in two before this head reached the tree. One could see its trail as trees were leveled to the ground."[9]

---

8. Jesse J. Cornplanter, *Legends of the Longhouse*, 86.
9. Ibid.

Sentinel Rock, Franklin County. Artist's conception of the eternal vigil that must be followed by the spirit of the disgraced Indian outlook that was cast into the rocks by the tribial shaman. (Drawing by James J. Frazier.)

The quaint story of the flying head certainly is entertaining to read, but it also makes it easy to think that if the Indians could have a legend about flying heads, they also could have a story about a derelict sentry's spirit being cast into a rock. In fact, this punishment of eternal vigilance would, no doubt, seem appropriate to them.

The unfortunate guard who had failed so miserably in doing his job would have gotten, in the minds of his contemporaries, just the punishment he deserved. In fact, Indian braves might have once used this story to teach their young men about responsibility, showing them the stone face on the mountain as an example of what could happen when a warrior didn't do his duty.

Note on the Indian face: In previous editions of Volume 3; the author noted he had tried on at least six separate occasions to find the sculpted face and the natural one whose photo appeared in the Gettysburg newspaper in 1900. Not being successful in either case, he declared that there "is another natural formation that passes for the Indian face today, but it is a poor imposter." He also stated that he had "given up looking for the original face after being warned that there had been sightings of a mountain lion on Caledonia Mountain some weeks before we had last been there."

EPILOGUE: In 2023, an avid South Mountain hiker and history buff contacted me to say that Sentinel Rock was "alive and well!" To support his contention, he provided photos that convinced me that the stone formation I had titled "The Great Imposter" in previous editions of Volume 3 might be the real McCoy after all. It appears that it's all a matter of getting into the correct position to view it, but it's difficult to know for sure, considering that over a hundred years have passed since the picture of Sentinel Rock appeared in the Gettysburg newspaper. The photos provided by the life-long Franklin County outdoorsman and scholar are included in this chapter so readers can decide for themselves.

CHAPTER 12

THE ENCHANTED
BULLET HOLE

Descriptions of the battles that took place during the Civil War often include references as to how intense the musket fire could be and, consequently, how thick the concentration of flying musket balls would get. Therefore, it's safe to say that the battle at Gettysburg on July 1st to 3rd, 1863, was not an exception to the rule, maybe even establishing some new standards in that regard. At least, there is one firsthand account that would seem to indicate that such a record was indeed established.

During the second day of the battle at Gettysburg, one soldier was so impressed by the condition of some of the slab fences along the Emmitsburg Road that he took some measurements. The wooden fence boards "were so completely perforated with bullet holes," he would later write, "that you could scarcely place a half-inch rule between them. One 1¼-inch thick board was indeed a curiosity. It was 16 feet long, 14 inches broad and was perforated with 836 musket balls."[1]

Nor was the Emmitsburg Road the only place where soldiers at Gettysburg experienced a devastating hail of bullets and one of the relics on display at the National Battlefield Park Visitor Center provides mute evidence of the deadly rain of fire that was sometimes common on the battlefield during the three-day battle. Shown in a museum display case are two musket balls that were found on the blood-soaked field after the clash

1. Gregory A. Coco, *On the Bloodstained Field*, 32.

Artist's depiction of Pickett's Charge. Mural of the famous charge that decided the Battle of Gettysburg. It can be seen inside the Cyclorama Visitors Center, Gettysburg National Military Park.

ended. The two Minié balls are fused together, apparently as a result of a mid-air collision.

There were, of course, soldiers in the midst of all these small messengers of death, and many men only survived because they had a large amount of luck. It almost seems that some men had charmed lives or the protection of a divine hand in order to have survived at all, and there's probably no better example of such fellows than "Snap" Rouser of Company K, Pennsylvania Reserves, a unit that would later be described as "the boys who fought at home."[2]

As a matter of fact, it was when they were fighting the Confederates around Little Round Top that Snap made the history books. Sometime in the midst of this particular skirmish, Rouser had the misfortune to get hit with a Rebel's Minié ball. Normally, a man would have been killed instantly if hit where Rouser got shot, but the young Federal was lucky.

---

2. Colonel Jacob M. Sheads (born 1910), recorded July 28, 1989.

Henry Meyer In full Civil War uniform. This picture was taken near Baltimore, Maryland, just as this young Rebersburg, Centre County, native was being sent off to war as a member of Company A, 148th Pennsylvania Volunteers. He would later fight at Chancellorsville, Gettysburg, and at Po River, where he lost his right hand. (Photo courtesy of Barbara Abbot.)

He is said to be the only known soldier in the entire Union army to have stopped a Minié ball with his front teeth. Rouser was lucky, certainly enough, considering there were 51,000 men who lost their lives during the same battle.

The fortunate soldier, if he survived the rest of the war, was probably always subsequently reminded of his amazing good luck when he smiled, because he must have had his front teeth knocked out when they stopped the Minié ball that would have surely killed him otherwise. But Rouser wasn't the only lucky soldier in the war. Others escaped death by margins just as narrow as his or by even narrower ones.

There were probably many veterans still alive 100 years ago who had experienced a close brush with death during the War Between the States, and each man might have considered his to be the closest. If so, then John Riter and Jacob Dunkle, both of Centre County, would have been top contenders for the honor.

Riter settled near Centre Hall, Centre County, after serving with a company of sharpshooters from Massachusetts during the war. In Centre County, he became a respected veterinarian, but his biggest claim to fame was probably the tales he could tell of his wartime experiences, including the story of the battle where he lost his eye.

At the Battle of Cold Harbor, June 30, 1864, Riter fought, he would say, "where the lead flew thickest."[3] It was a battle that ended as a terrible defeat for Union troops. It was a fight where Federals encountered such intense Rebel musket fire that Union lines were mowed down so quickly, one upon the other, one soldier would later describe it as being like "toppling dominoes."[4]

Riter may have been one of those dominoes, for he probably went down like a ton of bricks when a deadly greeting from the enemy lines "entered his left eye, and passed to a position back of his ear where it remained embedded in his brain."[5] Somehow, he survived his wound, but Riter carried the souvenir bullet and endured the constant pain caused by it for the rest of his life.

---

3. William W. Kerlin, *Centre Hall, Centre County, Pennsylvania*, 34.
4. Robert Leckie, *The Wars of America*, 497.
5. William W. Kerlin, *Centre Hall, Centre County, Pennsylvania*, 34.

Not too far down the valley from Riter, in the little village of Aaronsburg, lived a fellow soldier named Jacob Dunkle. Dunkle had been wounded in much the same way Riter had been, and perhaps the two men knew one another. If they were not acquainted before, then they surely must have spoken after Dunkle's coughing fit became a news item.

It seems that one day in 1894, Dunkle experienced such a harsh coughing spell that a doctor's services were required. Then, episodic repeats of these harsher spells occurred from time to time, until one day the Aaronsburg soldier coughed up the bullet that had been embedded in his brain all those years since the war. Jacob Dunkle survived this last wartime onslaught, but his unusual coughing fit must have impressed his doctor considerably, for it was later reported that "the bullet is now in possession of Dr. Frank of Millheim."[6]

Jacob Dunkle's bullet would have been an unusual relic of the Civil War, just as Snap Rouser's would have been if it had been saved, but there was also another bullet that was fired at Gettysburg, and its story is not one of hate, but one of love. Oftentimes, in narratives of the Civil War, descriptions of troop movements and battles dominate the text, and the human side of the war is forgotten. However, at Gettysburg, there is one human interest story about the battle that has never failed to interest anyone who has heard it. Nonetheless, many people, unless they've visited the Gettysburg house where the incident occurred, have never known about the rest of the story and the legend that it spawned.

During the battle at Gettysburg, many residents of the town remained in their homes because they felt certain that Confederate troops would never break through Union lines and enter Gettysburg itself, and two of those residents were Georgia McClellan and her sister, Mary Virginia Wade. Georgia's husband, John Lewis McClellan, was a Union soldier who was away at war on June 26, 1863, when Georgia gave birth to their first son.

It was the birth of Lewis Kenneth McClellan that prompted Mary Virginia, called Jennie by her friends and family, to move in with Georgia. Although Jennie must have known that the town was sandwiched between opposing armies, her desire to help her sister with the new baby and with

6. Ibid.

Civil War cannons at Gettysburg. Cannons like this can be seen all over the Gettysburg Battlefield, and it was guns like these that caused the air to reverberate like thunder during the great battle.

household chores overcame any fears she might have had about the struggle that was being waged on the outskirts of the community.

Sounds of that battle must have interrupted the long hours the two sisters spent together in the McClellan house on Baltimore Street, and Jennie and Georgia probably listened to those sounds as the fighting surged back and forth through places whose titles would become infamous because of the number of men who died there—names like the Peach Orchard, the Wheat Field, the Bloody Angle, and the "Slaughter Pen" at Devil's Den.

As they listened to the roar of the cannons and the firing of muskets, the women's thoughts and conversation also probably turned to their soldier boys. Georgia's husband was many miles from home and, for all she knew, was in the middle of a battle just like the one she was listening to at her front door. Jennie's thoughts at this same time were probably on her fiancé, Jack, Corporal Johnston H. Skelly, who was with the boys in blue somewhere in Virginia.

Jack Skelly and Jennie Wade had been sweethearts since they were kids, and several months before Jack had gone off to war he and Jennie had decided they would be married the next September. Not too long after his departure, the ever-faithful Skelly wrote to Jennie, and in his letter, he reaffirmed his undying love for her and his country. It was a letter that Jennie kept, but she would never get to tell her fiancé how much it meant to her.

The first day of the Battle of Gettysburg, July 1, had ended in the retreat of Union troops through the town, but Union reinforcements had arrived that night, and by July 2, they had established solid defenses on places like Seminary Ridge, Culp's Hill, and on the critical elevation called Little Round Top. When July 2 dawned, the little town of Gettysburg awoke to find that its eastern, northeastern, and southern sections were battlegrounds.

There might have been some residents who, on July 2, began to have some doubts about whether Gettysburg would be safe from southern invasion after all, but Jennie Wade and her sister must not have been among them. The two women went about their normal household routine, with Jennie settling in to bake bread in the kitchen.

It must have been the smell of that baking bread that led two Union soldiers passing by the McClellan house to stop and ask for food. Jennie could not refuse the hungry warriors, and she gave them each some bread from the first batch she had made that day and then returned to her second batch, which she began mixing in a baking tray. Perhaps the presence of the Union soldiers made Jennie and Georgia feel too secure or too confident, because even a stray bullet that entered a parlor window a short time later didn't stop Jennie from her appointed task. However, the young girl should have reflected upon the warning the bullet seemed to carry.

The stray missile did not fall harmlessly to the floor. Instead, it whizzed into the parlor and hit Mrs. McClellan's bedpost, falling right next to her head. Ironically enough, her bed had been moved to the parlor from her upstairs bedroom several days earlier, in order that she might recover from her childbirth more readily, but as she lay there that morning, she must have been too frightened to go back to sleep after the bullet came through the parlor window. If she didn't fall back to sleep at that point, then she

The snipers' window in the Farnsworth House. It was from this window that the Confederate snipers were shooting when one of their musket balls killed Jennie Wade. A close-up inspection reveals white pockmarks in the bricks, made by musket balls of Union troops returning fire.

most certainly heard another, more deadly, bullet crash through the inner and outer doors at the back of her house.

Some historians think that the bullet that entered the rear door of the McClellan house came from a Confederate sharpshooter who had been hiding in John Rupp's tannery across the street. The sharpshooter was most

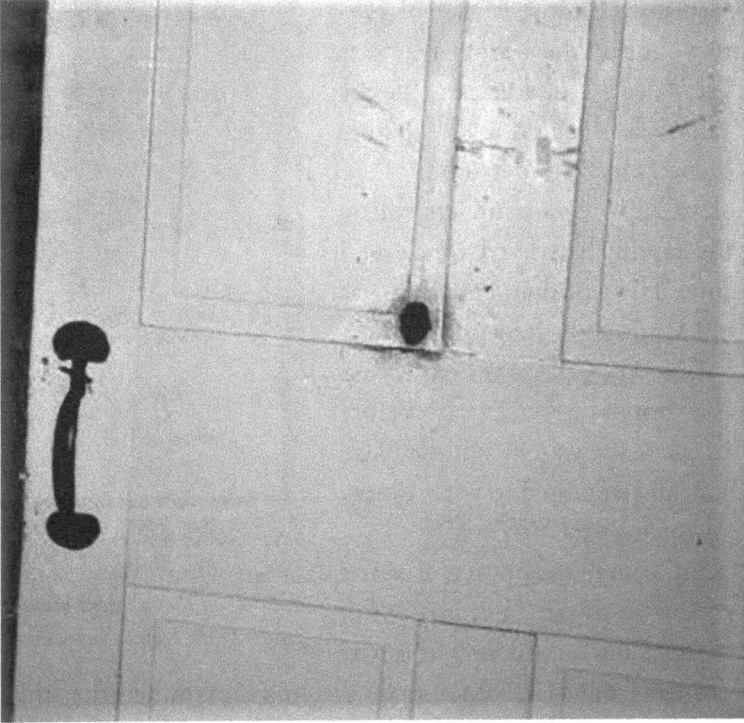

The enchanted bullet hole. Hole in the front door of the house made by the musket ball that killed Jennie Wade. It is this aperture that provide hope to ladies seeking their true love.

likely aiming at some Union soldiers, but his musket ball found another mark instead. The bullet that came through the house doors certainly would have made enough noise to frighten anyone, but Jennie probably didn't even have time enough to be startled.

After cleanly passing through the doors, the bullet hit the unsuspecting girl in the back, passed on through her body, came out her neck, and landed in the baking tray. She was killed instantly, an untimely end for a young lady whose life was filled with such hope and promise. However, Jenny's death became the basis for a legend that, at least in some peoples' minds, offers hope to others much like her.

There was also another native of Gettysburg whose fate would be determined by the battle there, and whose death would become inextricably entwined with that of Jennie Wade. Although his demise is filled with as

much pathos and irony as that of Jennie's, this young soldier's story is not as
widely heralded. Nonetheless, Wesley
Culp's tale must be told if the Jennie
Wade legend is to be understood.

Wesley Culp grew up in Gettysburg,
where his family had lived for several
generations. His grandfather's farm was
there, and Culp had often played there
as a boy. But Wes Culp was not swayed
by familial bonds. Several years before
the outbreak of the war, he left the place
of his birth and migrated to what is now
Shepherdstown, West Virginia.

Picture of Jennie Wade. Charcoal drawing of the innocent maid, in the Jennie Wade House, Gettysburg.

At that time the peaceful little
country hamlet was in Virginia. Still,
five years later, during the height of the
Civil War, the western inhabitants of Virginia determined that the bonds
of statehood were weaker than their northern sympathies. So, they seceded
from their home state to form the new state of West Virginia. However, by
that time, Wesley Culp was already committed to the Southern cause, and
he was clad in the grey uniform of a Rebel soldier.

Shortly after he had arrived in Shepherdstown, Culp's interests drew
him into a local militia unit that appealed to him because it seemed to be a
glamorous outlet for a young man's energies. War clouds were not yet gathering on the horizon, and the main business of the home guards appeared
to be providing young men a place to socialize and a way to impress the
local girls by marching around in dashing uniforms.

Appealing incentives like this were probably the main reason that Wesley signed up with the guards, and he most likely enjoyed the camaraderie
for a while. However, the young troopers' fun turned into serious business
on the day the call to war finally came, and the soldiers, to a man, joined
the Confederate Army.

Oblivious to the horrors that real war would bring, Wesley Culp's
guard unit was placed in a Virginia regiment that would, after the first

Battle of Bull Run in July 1861, become known as the Stonewall Brigade because of their spirited and successful defense in the face of overwhelming enemy troops during that engagement. It was a name they took with them to Gettysburg two years later.

Their march toward Pennsylvania in 1863 was not eventful until they neared Winchester, Virginia, where they encountered and fought with Federal forces at that place. Ironically enough, those boys in blue were troops that had been recruited in Gettysburg, and among them was a man who had been one of Wes Culp's best boyhood chums. After the battle was over, Culp somehow learned that his friend had been wounded, and he managed to find him among the casualties.

The wounded corporal's main concern was that his sweetheart in Gettysburg be told of his whereabouts, and Culp agreed that if he ever got back to that place, he would deliver the message to the girl, whose name was Jennie Wade. Later that night, when Jack Skelly died of his wounds on that Virginia battlefield, which later would be assigned dual names (it was referred to as Bull Run by the North and Manassas by the South), he probably expired thinking that at least his betrothed would know that his last thoughts were of her.

When the Stonewall Brigade did finally reach Gettysburg the landscape that spread out before them must have been familiar to Wes Culp. Scenes of his boyhood probably came flooding into his mind as his brigade marched past familiar farms and fields, but he most certainly was surprised when they were ordered to dig in on an elevation that was once part of his grandfather's farm.

It was the same hill he had romped upon as a youngster, perhaps making pretend charges here when he played army with his friends. The irony of the situation could not have escaped him when he realized that he was about to fight a real battle near the little knoll, which still bore his family's name.

Any visions of boyhood pleasures that Wes Culp had on Culp's Hill that day must have been short-lived. The reality of the moment would have crowded out any pleasurable thoughts, prompting this dedicated young soldier to remember his promise to Jack Skelly. One tale says that Culp actually sent a message to Jennie Wade's mother, asking her to meet him

Statue of Jennie Wade. It stands just outside the Jennie Wade House in Gettysburg.

the next day, but it was a meeting that was not to be. On July 2nd, Wesley Culp paid the supreme sacrifice. He died on Culp's Hill, defending the place where he had experienced the joys of childhood.

"So, the message he had for this woman didn't matter," explained the former park ranger who was an expert on the human-interest stories of the conflict at Gettysburg, "because the woman who was Skelly's fiancée

The star-crossed lovers. Rare tintypes of, left to right, Wesley Culp, Jennie Wade, and Jack Skelly.

was Jennie Wade, and Jennie was the only civilian killed in the battle. And when they carried her body through the house to the other side, a photograph, a little daguerreotype, of Skelly fell out of her pocket.

"We're really not sure if she had an engagement ring or anything like that, whatever they did back in those days, but maybe the only people who knew she was engaged would have been Culp, Skelly, and Jennie. Nevertheless, it's kind of an odd coincidence. All three died without knowing the others' fate."[7]

Visitors that come to the Gettysburg battlefield today often visit the former McClellan home on Baltimore Street. Here, they are shown throughout the structure, which still looks almost like it did on that fateful day in 1863. The kitchen where Jennie was baking her bread has been authentically reproduced, right down to the baking tray. Upstairs, Jennie's picture is hanging on the wall of one of the bedrooms, and it silently yet eloquently expresses the innocence and sweetness that must have been a dominant part of her personality.

However, the one major piece of the house that has been carefully protected throughout the years and which most eloquently bears silent witness to the sad thing that happened here on that July day in 1863 is the outside

7. Mark Nesbitt, recorded August 28, 1988.

door with the bullet hole. It is this bullet hole that is the foundation for the legend that clings to the house on Baltimore Street.

If someone didn't know the legend, they would wonder why the bullet hole is now smoothly polished all around and much larger than it must have been originally. The explanation for the bullet hole's condition today rests with the legend which states that if an unmarried girl inserts her finger into the hole, she will, within a year, receive a marriage proposal.

No explanations as to the origin of this quaint belief seem to be apparent, but it's not hard to guess that someone who knew the saga of Jennie's unfulfilled love, and perhaps knew Jennie herself, created the myth. On the other hand, the legend may just have been invented by a savvy owner in order to attract paying tourists. In any case, the fable of the bullet hole's powers does seem to be based on Jennie's tragic love story, and some put unquestioning faith in the legend's claims.

At least one young lady once felt that the legend had special significance in her life, assuming that the following letter on display in the house was genuine. Since the missive is dated July 4, 1976, there were probably many other young ladies over the years who were just as convinced as the writer of the following epistle that their matrimonial successes were aided by the powers of the bullet hole:

> Sir, I must tell you my story. You have told the superstition about the bullet hole in the door many times. And all young ladies would declare they are not superstitious. So, of course, neither am I. But half in fun and whole earnest, the particular finger is usually thrust into the hole. I have an awfully good excuse. It was at Easter time we brought our Girl Scouts to your house on our way to Washington. And since the spell doesn't work on girls under twenty-one, I put my finger in to please them.
>
> That sounds reasonable, doesn't it? Secretly, I hoped but sincerely felt that it wouldn't possibly happen. Now, you have probably guessed the result, if you wish to call it that. In May, he drove 650 miles to see me (I had never expected to see him again). We decided we were deeply in love. He proposed. My diamond ring is to come this week—for my birthday. And the wedding will be no later than the next spring. I assure you the story is true in every detail. I still won't admit I am superstitious. But

perhaps you are more definitely justified in leading others' faith to hope.
May others find similar happiness.

Sincerely, Alma.[8]

Although Jennie Wade's life ended tragically, and she never had the opportunity to fulfill her destiny with the man she loved, she nonetheless might be satisfied with what has been done with her story. She would, no doubt, be happy to know that her sad tale is the basis for a legend that now seems to be a source of hope to young girls much like her.

---

8. Copied from the letter on display at the Jennie Wade House on Baltimore Street in Gettysburg, (used by permission).

CHAPTER 13

FIDDLING PHANTOMS

People up in Indiana County's Mahoning Valley still remember the house of the fiddling ghost. Although the odd-looking structure burned down under mysterious circumstances about forty years ago, the place is still recalled when folks in Smicksburg talk about spooks and other things that are apt to send chills up a person's spine.

The old residence was always considered different due to its unusual architecture, but according to legend, it wasn't until a murder occurred there, around the time that the tracks were being laid for the Rochester and Pittsburgh Railroad, that the house really became a popular object of curiosity.

The railroad, which was later to become part of the Baltimore and Ohio rail system, would open up an area that had been isolated for centuries. In fact, northern Indiana County was still at that same time referred to as territory "up above the purchase,"[1] a throwback to 1768 when the Penn family bought (many would say cheated away) from the Indians that part of northern Pennsylvania that lies above a line running from Cherry Tree, Indiana County, to Kittanning, Armstrong County.

That purchase was the last that the Penns made from the Indians, and so the lands north of the purchase line were among the last in the state to be fully settled. Once as common a phrase in Indiana County as the Mason and Dixon Line is to those in southern Pennsylvania, the term Purchase

---

1. George Swetnam, "The Fiddling Ghost of Mahoning Valley," article which appeared in *The Pittsburgh Press* on October 30, 1955. See also: John Blair Linn, *History of Centre and Clinton Counties*, 584.

Portrait of Ole Borneman Bull as a young man.

Line is preserved today in the name of an Indiana County town that lies on the original purchase boundary.

About twenty miles above the Indian purchase line and close to where Mahoning Creek intersects the Baltimore and Ohio tracks, there is a township road near the town of Smicksburg that is called Rossmoyne Road. The highway has only been paved within the last couple of decades, and so the area was not well-traveled for some time. However, there may just have been another reason for the lack of traffic through here over the years, and that reason might be because not too far off Rossmoyne Road, along a dusty country road, once sat a home known to locals as the house of the fiddling ghost.

Early Ole Bull postcard. Shows the castle retaining wall and the great violinist with violin in hand. (Copy courtesy of the Potter County Historical Society.)

There is just a vacant lot there now, the charred remains of the old house bulldozed away by the edict of the township authorities some years ago. Nonetheless, the story of the place still lives on in the memory of those who know the legend, and perhaps the notes from the ghostly fiddler can still be heard as well if passersby listen closely.

However, the possibility of hearing his music probably depends on whether one believes in such things or not. On the other hand, it's interesting to note that this legend is similar to that of another, more famous, fiddling ghost in the state. It also has its counterparts in Europe, where ghostly musicians have entertained people for centuries.

The Mahoning Valley legend of the fiddling ghost begins at the time when two men, apparently not related, came to the valley to help lay tracks for the Rochester and Pittsburgh Railroad. The two railroad workers bought or rented a house to live in near Smicksburg; a place considered to be rather odd-looking at that time. Surprisingly, the architecture was probably a bit ahead of its time since it was more like what we would call an A-frame today. However, despite any modern appearances the place might have exhibited, there was a decidedly old-timey aspect to one of its inhabitants.

According to the legend, one of the men living in the house was, in some ways, a bit of a throwback to an earlier period. It is said that he was an old-time fiddler who was so talented that he was often asked to play at barn dances and other social events. The local story doesn't state whether or not the fiddler liked to boast about his skills, but if he was as good as the legend states, then he might have at least been forgiven if he boosted his skills to the extent that legendary traditional country fiddler "Uncle" Dave Macon once touted his.

"I can fiddle taters off the vine" was Uncle Dave's claim to fame, and undoubtedly, the Mahoning Valley fiddler would have been a regular at any fiddle playing contests held in the area if he was anywhere as good as Uncle Dave. However, anyone that talented did not get and stay that way without lots of practice.

It takes hours and hours of repetition, day after day, to become a great fiddler, and that is probably why the old Mahoning Valley legend claims that it was rehearsal like this that may have led to a murder. Perhaps the incessant sound of a fiddle gradually grated upon the nerves of the other resident of the odd-looking house.

The second man may not have appreciated fine old fiddle tunes as much as his companion, and the constant music may have been too much. After hearing repeated renditions of tunes like "The Lop-eared Mule," "Over the Stump and Back Again," or others similar to those collected by Samuel Bayard in Greene County in the 1940s,[2] the non-fiddler may have snapped. At least the legend considers him to be a prime suspect in the death of his friend.

According to that story, one day, neither man showed up for work at the railroad. Later on that day, when people came to the house to look for the men, they found the fiddler stabbed to death, his fiddle broken to bits, and the fiddle bow snapped in half. The second man was not found and was never seen again.

Eventually, the sensational occurrence became less of a topic in the valley, but rumors about the house persisted. Tales began to surface about people who saw strange things as they passed by the deserted place on nights of a full moon when there was an icy nip in the air and hoary frost on the ground. On such nights, there seemed to be, so said the tales,

2. Samuel P. Bayard, *Hill Country Tunes*, 56, 66.

OLE BULL'S CASTLE
Presented to
Annie Halenbake Ross Library
BY
HENRY W. SHOEMAKER,
Author of Pennsylvania Mountain Stories

The castle that never was. Painting by C. H. Sharer is an imaginative view of what the artist thought Ole Bull's castle would have looked like had it ever been built. The painting, donated by Henry W. Shoemaker and much in need of cleaning, hangs in the Annie E. Ross Library in Lock Haven.

a ghostly white vapor clinging to the peak of the house's steep roof. If observed long enough, swore those who had seen it, the swirling mists eventually coalesced into the form of the murdered fiddler, who appeared to be sitting up there and playing his instrument. Those who were brave enough to stay and watch claimed that they could even sometimes hear the ghostly strains of the fiddler's music.

The castle site. All that is left of the place where Bull's log cabin was built, and the historic marker telling the story that it was here where his castle was to stand.

Today, the house of the fiddling ghost is gone, and those who know the legend are disappearing as well. However, there may be others who read this story and decide, on some frosty night when the moon is full, to visit the vacant lot where the house of the fiddling ghost once stood. They will, no doubt, hope to see the ghost or at least hear the strains of some old fiddle tune like "Hell's Broke Loose in Smicksburg." However, before they go to the trouble, they should read on and learn about the tale of another fiddling ghost.

Anyone who has heard of Ole Bull State Park in Potter County has probably wondered about this man for whom the park was named. This lack of enduring fame would probably sadden Ole Bull, for in his day, he was an international celebrity.

Bull was born in Norway in 1810, eventually becoming a violin virtuoso whose concert tours throughout Europe, Canada, the West Indies, and the United States were greeted with enthusiasm. Even the great violinist Paganini was impressed with Ole Borneman Bull's technique, and the Norwegian's fame preceded him when he returned to the United States in 1852 for another concert tour.

But Ole Bull had another reason for returning to this country in 1852; he wanted to look for land here, too; in his own words, he "found a new Norway, consecrated to liberty, baptized with independence, and protected by the Union's mighty flag."[3] Discouraged by Sweden's subjugation of his native country, as dictated by a settlement made at the Congress of Vienna in 1815, the patriotic young musician wanted to create a place of freedom for his fellow countrymen who were as disillusioned as he was with the constraints placed upon them by the new aristocracy.

As he pursued his dream, the idealistic young Norwegian was eventually introduced to John F. Cowan of Williamsport, who "sold" Bull 11,000 acres of land along Kettle Creek in that part of Pennsylvania's North Woods known as the Black Forest. The territory and climate there appealed to Bull because it reminded him of his native Norway, and so he began to build his colony in earnest. Eventually, a great stone castle "of feudal proportions"[4] was envisioned for the great master's residence, and the towns of New Norway, New Bergen, Oleona, and Walhalla were also planned.

Norwegian settlers attacked the wilderness they called "Ole Bull's Promised Land" with a vengeance, but the land was never meant for farming, and the progress was slow. Nevertheless, the number of settlers gradually increased, peaking at 800 in 1853, until they learned their leader had been duped.

The lands that Cowan had sold Bull were not lands that Cowan owned, which was not surprising to those who knew the speculator as someone of dubious integrity. Said one man who had dealt with this shady character, "I would as soon pick the bait out of a steel trap as to have any dealings with him!"[5]

Ole Bull's colony fell apart after Cowan's land scheme came to light. The great castle overlooking Kettle Creek was never completed, and the State Department of Forestry eventually dismantled the massive stone walls that had been erected. Today, only the town of Oleona still lives on to commemorate the ambitious dreams of the young violinist who inspired so many with his music. Descriptions of that music have come down to us

3. John T. Faris, *Seeing Pennsylvania*, 193.
4. Ibid., 194.
5. Norman B. Wilkinson, "Ole Bull's New Norway," *Historic Pennsylvania Leaflet Number 14*, 4.

over the years, and they preserve a flavor of just how inspiring the violinist must have been when he got out his Stradivarius and began to play.

"It was the finest music I ever heard,"[6] recalled W. H. Sanderson, who heard Bull play at the Jersey Shore High School in 1862. And a similar testimony came down from Warren Wycoff, noted guide and big game hunter of the Cross Fork area of Potter County during the 1920s and '30s.

Wycoff's father had heard Bull play, and the master's music even touched the heart of this roughhewn backwoodsman. "Bull's music made you see the scenes the music was written about,"[7] was the way the old mountaineer would later describe the notes he had heard.

It was a surprising comment coming from someone not usually prone to such lofty thoughts, but Bull's music apparently had similar effects on many folks. "He could," claimed one of them, "reproduce the rush and roar of rapid streams, the frolic of the winds through the rocky glens, and the tempest's crash on the mountaintop!"[8]

Regardless of his great talent and his many critically acclaimed successes in the concert halls of the world, Ole Bull was emotionally and financially ruined by his misdealings with John Cowan. It is said that when he realized his dreams had been shattered, "the prince of violinists" went mad, "wandering off into the mountains half-crazy with grief and playing his violin far into the night." Then, before recovering his composure and returning to his beloved castle, "he broke the instrument and buried it in the hillside."[9] (See the chapter titled "Ole Bull's Castle" in the author's *Pennsylvania Mountain Landmarks Volume 2* for more details about Ole Bull and his settlements in Potter County).

The Ole Bull legend has grown over the years and, as is common with many such tales, has even taken on some supernatural aspects. Today, so states the current version of the legend, campers and hikers who find themselves near the violinist's castle site will, on certain days of the year, when winds whistle gently in the trees and water splashes gently over the rocks in the stream below, hear the "faint sounds of Beethoven's Eighth Sonata."[10]

---

6. Thomas W. Lloyd, *Ole Bull in Pennsylvania*, 38.

7. James Gates (born 1905), interviewed September 27, 1978.

8. John T. Faris, *Seeing Pennsylvania*, 194.

9. Norman B. Wilkinson, "Ole Bull's New Norway," *Historic Pennsylvania Leaflet Number 14*, 3.

10. "You've Got a Ghost in Pennsylvania," Pennsylvania Bureau of Travel Development, fall press release of unknown date.

The Fiddling Ghost of Mahoning Valley. Artist's depiction of how the once-famous Indiana County ghost may have appeared to those who claimed to have seen it. Appeared in The Pittsburgh Express *on 10/30/1955.*

It is, say the believers, Ole Bull's spirit still playing on his beloved violin. But there are other places where ghostly music like this has been heard as well, and that causes us to wonder if the tale is just another variety of the urban legends so popular today. Indiana County's Mahoning Valley can claim one such tale, of course, but there are many castles in Europe where similar tales once abounded.

One of the most famous haunted castles like this in Great Britain is Cortachy Castle, the ancestral home of the Earls of Airlie. Here, it was once believed that the sound of a ghostly drummer often foretold "the speedy death of a member of the Ogilvie family."[11]

Legend has it that the ghost is that of a drummer who had incurred the wrath of a previous Lord Airlie, who ordered that the drummer was to be stuffed into his drum and thrown out of one of the castle's tower windows. It is the vengeful ghost of this murdered drummer, so says the legend, that reminds the Ogilvies of the black mark in their history whenever one of them is about to die.

There are certainly many other examples of musical ghosts in the British Isles, the harper of Inveraray Castle being another fine example, and so the storyline is an old one. Nonetheless, it is a fascinating one for those who enjoy the ancient and the mysterious.

It is indeed fun to speculate on the possibility of such things actually happening, but those of a less romantic mindset probably prefer to look at these things in the same light as the gentleman from Smicksburg, who, when I asked him about the fiddling ghost and ghosts in general, replied "They're about all died off. The new generation don't keep up with them. You see, now they have television. They have all that horror stuff on there instead of telling these good stories around the table in the evening."[12]

---

11. John H. Ingram, *Haunted Homes and Family Traditions of Great Britain*, 4.
12. Robert Lockhart (born 1932), recorded December 28, 1997.

CHAPTER 14

NIGHT SCREAMS

Chickies Rock County Park in Lancaster County has gained a reputation over the decades as one of the most haunted sections in the entire state. It seems that every year, a new ghost story or another episode of the supernatural is told about the scenic region that overlooks the Susquehanna River and the Hellam Hills near the town of Columbia. Several interesting collections of these tales have been published in recent years; those by local author Dorothy Fiedel being among the most complete. However, despite her diligent efforts, Fiedel still hasn't managed to preserve all the singular stories of the region, including the curious tale of the haunted railroad tunnel.

Perhaps the reason for that is because the story appears to be a perfect example of how someone takes some real history and uses it to explain what to them appear to be supernatural events. At least that's what the descendants of Michael Keppler believe has happened in this case, but some of the rangers at Chickies Park, on the other hand, are convinced that Keppler's untimely end offers a perfect explanation for the uncanny events now occurring where he died in the waning years of the nineteenth century.

Michael Keppler's mangled remains were discovered in the old railroad tunnel that once served as a passageway for the train that carried materials to and from the large iron furnaces located nearby. Legend and history differ markedly on how Keppler ended up in that tunnel just outside the iron manufactory, and so this part of the legend remains shrouded in mystery. However, the Henry Clay Iron Works was once a real place, and there's no doubt about that.

*Chickies Furnace No. 2, formerly Eagle Furnace, opened in the Marietta area in 1855.
This Columbia Historic Preservation Society photo appears in Frederic H. Abendschein's
"Columbia, Marietta, and Wrightsville" (Arcadia Press, 2009). Photo caption states:
"Nicknamed the 'happy face building' because of the appearance with windows for eyes,
a round window nose, and a door mouth, the building is one of the few remaining
structures from that era."*

Situated along the Susquehanna between the river towns of Marietta
and Columbia, the Clay Works was once a major employer in this part
of Lancaster County. No definite explanation for the facility's name seems
to have come down to the present day, but the owner must have been an
admirer of Congressman Henry Clay, one of the most highly respected pol-
iticians in America during the years immediately preceding the Civil War.

Despite the fame of the person for whom it was named, most people
today don't seem to realize that such a place as the Henry Clay Furnace
even existed here along the scenic Susquehanna. There are few traces left of
the original plant, and even though the old railroad bed that the rail tracks
were laid upon can still be seen, the steel rails that once led to the furnace
have been gone for years.

However, there are other tracks, those of the Conrail system, that still
lie along the river here, stretching under Route 30 and passing by the old
rail yards in Columbia. Looking in the opposite direction, to the north
toward Chickies Rock and Marietta, the keen observer will also see remains
of a furnace—part of the original Henry Clay complex.

Those who pause a little longer to look upriver toward the impressive ledge known as Chickies Rock may also notice the dark and mysterious entrance to the tunnel that was painstakingly carved out of the solid rock face of Chickies Ridge. It is this same tunnel that serves as the setting for the chilling events that are preserved in the legend of this place. It is a legend, so say some of the local rangers, which begins with an architect who was educated at Heidelberg University in the ancient West German city of Heidelberg.

According to the legend as it's told today, the architect, one Michael Keppler, decided to immigrate to this country sometime in the late 1800s. Keppler, it is said, brought his wife and children along with him in order to find a better life, but that dream was never to be realized.

The legend claims that there was no employment for architects in the section of Pennsylvania where Keppler settled, especially architectural jobs for those as highly educated as he was. Therefore, in order to support his family, Keppler had to take a menial spot as a laborer at the Henry Clay Iron Works along the mighty Susquehanna.

Working close to a hot and dirty iron furnace every day, seven days a week for twelve hours a day, was an insult to someone educated in a prestigious seat of learning like that at Heidelberg, and this preyed upon his mind, eventually changing him from a positive and genial person to one who was negative and argumentative. Michael Keppler became more and more irascible and hard to live with as time wore on, and he eventually tried to drown his desperation in bouts of prolonged drinking.

But alcohol only made matters worse, and Keppler's friends no longer wanted to associate with him. His wife, too, eventually had enough, and she finally kicked him out of their house.

The forsaken husband had no choice at that point but to move into the company houses at the ironworks and live in cramped quarters with the other ironworkers. This proved to be the last straw, and the once-genial architect was now apt to get angry over even smaller things than before.

Even his drinking became more intense, and so, on the rare nights off from the fiery pits where he made his living, he could often be seen, sometimes with a bottle in his hand, staggering off to one of the many watering holes in Columbia. It was this combination of anger and liquor that ultimately led to his undoing, for Keppler was now apt to erupt at the slightest provocation, and so was often one of the combatants in any fights that broke out in the bars in Columbia.

These are the background details presented in the legend that is told about Michael Keppler today, and they set the stage for the next part of the account that describes how Keppler met his untimely end. According to this segment of the story, one night, when Keppler was staggering off to one of his favorite drinking spots, he passed by the night watchmen who stood guard at the gates to the iron complex.

They pleasantly bid him a good night, but he did not answer in kind, cursing at them instead. Later, in the wee small hours of the morning, these same watchmen saw Keppler returning, but not on foot. Instead, he was driving a horse and buggy, which was a bit of a mystery to the men. The rig was a fancy outfit, one that was too expensive for someone of Keppler's limited means.

However, Keppler ignored their stares and, despite their warnings, drove right into the railroad tunnel. Within minutes, the watchmen heard the train whistle and then the "screams and shrieks of a man being shredded underneath the locomotive."[1]

The legend, as it's told now, does not end with Keppler's death. Instead, the account goes on to speculate about how this man of decidedly modest means ended up with a fancy horse and buggy. Did he steal it and, in a drunken state, mistakenly drive into the tunnel, or did something more sinister happen? Perhaps someone forced him to drive the buggy into the tunnel where they could rob and murder him and then lay his body on the tracks so the train would run him over.

It would have been a good way to confuse those who later tried to ascertain the cause of death, but whatever the case, the legendary accounts say that Keppler's spirit is a restless one due to his untimely and violent end. It is Keppler's spirit that haunts this place, or so say some of those who have had otherworldly experiences in the deteriorating Clay Works tunnel.

"Misfortune is often bestowed upon people who travel through that tunnel," claims one park ranger who has experienced some weird events there himself. "I don't know that I believe in all these things, but I did have

---

1. Luke Brackett, recorded July 19, 1997.

View of Heidelberg Germany. Taken from the walls of Heidelberg Castle by the author in September of 1998.

a few experiences of my own. Twice in one week, my Jeep got a flat tire when I was driving through that tunnel.

"Other than being a little bit upset at having to sit in the train yard changing tires while eight or ten Conrail workers kind of looked at me and laughed, I didn't think a whole lot of it. Then, a week later, when driving through that tunnel, almost to the hour, I got a flat tire in the exact same tire, but I just assumed that there was something in the bottom of this big puddle that forms there in the spring that was causing my tires to go flat."

The memory of the flat tires would not leave his mind, and so, after a prolonged dry spell that dried up the water in the tunnel, the ranger decided to take a closer look. "I must've spent twenty or thirty minutes combing the bottom of that tunnel looking for anything I might've driven over that would give me a flat tire," explained the ranger, "but I didn't find it!"[2] The mystery of the flat tires might have ended there, but something else occurred that seemed even more eerie.

"The very last thing happened just a few weeks ago," continued the young man. "At that point I didn't know this story about Michael Keppler. I was going through the tunnel at about 9:30 P.M., and I thought I heard

---

2. Luke Brackett, recorded July 19, 1997.

voices. I'm not one who usually takes to hearing voices, so I thought there was a reasonable explanation for this.

"I walked to the other end of the tunnel, and I just assumed people were walking on the property above me. But it was odd; I heard a man's voice, but no one was answering him. I couldn't locate the source of the voice, and I didn't find any cars parked down there, so I haven't been real anxious to go back looking either! I'm not ready yet to say it was the spirit of Mr. Keppler, but if I don't find something soon, I might start to become a believer!"[3]

Although there may be logical explanations for the young ranger's tunnel experience, these types of peculiar events are perfect raw materials for the factories of the legendary world. The result of combining these ingredients with the story of Michael Keppler's murder results in the perfect ghost story. Nonetheless, the nagging questions and doubts remain. Was there such a man as Michael Keppler, and if so, are some of the man's biographical details preserved in the legend about the tunnel? It turns out that the answer to both questions is yes.

If Michael Keppler's spirit is a restless one, it may be because of the circumstances surrounding his unexplained death, which still leaves his descendants dissatisfied. On the other hand, he may be restless because of the way the legend has sullied his name by portraying him as a drunk and a thief. This second possibility doesn't rest well with his descendants either, and they are anxious to set the record straight.

Michael Keppler was a real person. Born in Bavaria in 1838, he was educated as an architect at Heidelberg University, just as the legend states. He immigrated to this country just prior to the Civil War, finding some employment here as an architect and builder. However, the work was sporadic, and he did some unique things to supplement his income.

"He was known as 'the old house mover,'" explained Keppler's great-great-granddaughter. "He used to move structures with block and tackle and mules with equipment he developed himself to do this. As far as the drinking goes, he was a typical German. They were hardworking and hard-drinking people; the majority of them drank. There wasn't such a word as alcoholism, and so he liked his booze."[4]

3. Ibid.
4. Dorothy Fiedel, recorded January 30, 1998.

It seems, however, that people actually regarded Keppler with some degree of respect. "The obituary in the paper said he was a nice fella and was well-liked by everyone," continued the family historian who had done some research on the matter. "Apparently he was highly thought of, and maybe he was looked at with a little bit of awe because he did have an education.

"In those days, very few people ever got out of eighth grade, if they did go to school at all! And he wasn't a vagrant. He took care of his family, and he fixed things around the house. At the time of his death, he was working at the Clay Furnace. Exactly what he was doing, I don't know, but he lived in the tenant house because things apparently at home weren't all 'hunky-dory.' So, it's not a happy story, but it's a human one.

"Well, apparently, according to the newspaper, he had borrowed, *borrowed*, not *stolen*; he had borrowed somebody's wagon and team of horses, and he went into town to have himself a few beers at a local pub. There were watchmen at the gate that led back to the Clay Furnace, and they saw him go out and talk to him. Everybody knew him, and they saw him come back, and they said, 'Hey, you'd better be careful. You've had a little too much to drink!'

"Well, whatever; he went on down the tracks, and they didn't hear anything from him, and then they found out he had been hit by a train. They didn't find the wagon or the horses, and they had an inquest into this death. They concluded that he had fallen off the wagon and had gotten run over by a train, but they didn't find any money in his pockets, and he always had money!"[5]

The suspicion that Michael Keppler had been robbed and then murdered on that sultry evening of July 12, 1893, plagued his children until they died. His granddaughter always stated that "momma and poppa always thought that maybe he was murdered, and his great-great-grand-daughter agrees. "Hey, maybe this guy was robbed and killed," she speculates. "Somebody might have hit him over the head!"[6]

Michael Keppler was "buried in pieces"[7] in the Mount Bethel Cemetery in Columbia. However, some years later, when declining upkeep gave this city of the dead a decidedly rundown look, his descendants had his

5. Ibid.
6. Ibid.
7. Ibid.

Entrance to the haunted railroad tunnel. Chickies Rock Park, Lancaster County, Pa.

remains exhumed and reinterred in Laurel Hill Memorial Park near the Columbia High School.

Although legendary lore states that a restless spirit is sometimes created when its body is reburied in the ground that is not pleasing to the dead person, it can only be hoped that this has not disturbed poor Michael Keppler. He seems to have had enough trouble when he was alive, and now, he should at least be allowed a peaceful existence while in the next world. Perhaps this small account, by setting the record somewhat straight, will help in that regard. However, there is still the matter of those flat tires.

Sometimes, following one of those days in July and August we call dog days, a warmer-than-usual night wind blows down from the Hellam Hills and across the cool waters of the nearby Susquehanna, causing dense mists to rise off the river's surface. The thicker the mists, the more surreal the area becomes, especially when the fog forms a deathly white shroud over the Conrail tracks and seeps into the deserted railroad tunnel that once seemed to glow from the coals of the steam engines traveling to and from the Henry Clay Furnace. The atmosphere seems surreal at such times, and perhaps that's why the odd tales persist. The ranger whose tires went flat, for example, may be glad to know that he's not alone in having such troubles.

In one of her several books on the uncanny tales of the area, Dorothy Fiedel tells the story of two couples who decided to have a picnic at Chickies Park in July of 1995. The young people decided to have their outing after dark, so that they could look for ghosts. However, the picnickers found out that it's really more fun to read about such things than actually to experience them firsthand.

The details of that evening are recounted in Fiedel's book, but unexplainable flat tires were among the hair-raising events of that night. When the couples discovered the first flat, they replaced it with the spare tire. However, after they had cooked their supper (a task which was also fraught with problems), and eaten, they discovered that the spare was now flat also.

Flat tires can be attributed to many normal causes, but in this case, after the tires went flat, there were accompanying events, according to those who were there at the time, that were decidedly abnormal. Probably the most frightening occurrences that night were the screams that suddenly emanated from the nearby woods and then the ball of mist that formed on the adjoining hillside and began rolling toward the picnickers.

As if that were not enough to send chills up the stiffest spine, the frightened couples then noticed that the air temperature had dropped considerably, and the nearby trees began swaying as though being swept by a violent blast of wind, even though the air was deathly calm.

It could, of course, be argued that the picnickers let their imaginations get the best of them that July night in 1995. Mists do roll off the river on such nights, and everyone does get flat tires at odd times and places and, we might add, at the most inconvenient times. Moreover, many times, those flat tires are caused by normal objects that cannot be found embedded in the tires when they are inspected.

However, as far as the flat tires at Chickies Rock and the uncanny events that seem to accompany them, many people, I think, will decide not to investigate firsthand. Most folks probably feel the same way as the ranger who wasn't "real anxious to go back looking" or like one of the picnickers who says, "Don't be at Chickies Rock after dark!"[8]

8. Dorothy Fiedel, *Ghosts and Other Mysteries*, 25.

CHAPTER 15

HAND TO HORN COMBAT

According to many old hunters who passed their stories on to me and whose lives stretched back into the latter part of the nineteenth century, there were a number of years during that period when the whitetail deer was a rarity in Pennsylvania. Sometime around the turn of that century, the whitetails were so scarce that, claimed one old veteran of the chase, "you couldn't even see a doe or a buck!"[1]

Moreover, in some sections of the state, this condition lasted until at least 1910 or later, a situation that often caused hunters to get excited when even the slightest signs of a deer were found. It is said that in those years prior to the 1920s, a deer hoof print was an object of curiosity in many parts of the state.

"Children would walk miles just to see a deer track!"[2] claimed yet another elderly nimrod and rare imprints like this would inspire hunters to get out their best tracking hounds in hopes of bagging a big buck. With the advent of the Roaring Twenties, however, the white-tailed deer became a more common sight in Pennsylvania forests.

Some said the turnaround was due to extensive lumbering operations that had begun in Virginia, the theory being that the deer there were driven northward because of the destruction of their habitat to the south. Although this suggestion could explain some of the increase in Pennsylvania's deer population around that time, it may have been an idea based

1. Paul Bartges, interviewed August 28, 1972.
2. Reverend Lawrence Bair (born 1920), recorded November 2, 1989.

more on denial than on fact. There is indeed another possible explanation for the rebirth of the deer herd in Pennsylvania around the first decades of the twentieth century, and it has to do more with a decrease in hunting excesses rather than with ambitious lumber kings.

Prior to 1900, there were no game laws in Pennsylvania, and for some time after the laws were passed, many veteran hunters chose to ignore them. The new restrictions took some getting used to, and even those who enforced them occasionally appeared to look the other way. At least that was the perception of many of the law-abiding hunters, who claimed that the wardens "wouldn't prosecute unless they had to."[3]

The honest hunters knew who the outlaws were, and some felt that the game wardens should know that as well. However, the reason officials chose to overlook the violators was not a mystery in the minds of the locals, who subscribed to a "relative" explanation for the lack of action on the part of the wardens.

Family ties were quite extensive in the sparsely populated rural areas of that day, and the fact that, as one man put it, "everyone was related in some way"[4] made it likely that a hunting rogue and a game warden were at least distant cousins. Although it was his duty to arrest anyone who broke a game law, a warden may have indeed decided on occasions that it would be far wiser not to do so rather than to incur the wrath of mutual friends and close-knit relatives.

On the other hand, it wouldn't have taken too many game offenders to make a noticeable difference in game populations, and so overkill was probably at least a contributing factor that kept the deer herd at minimal levels until the game laws began to be enforced more strictly. However, in some cases, the deer did manage, or at least appeared to try, to fight back, seemingly in an attempt to even the score with those they perceived as their executioners.

Old-time deer hunter Jackson Stover, who lived in the tiny mountain village of Coburn near the confluence of Elk and Penn's Creeks in Centre County, had the misfortune to shoot one such deer sometime during those first two decades of the twentieth century when the deer population here

3. Paul Bartges, interviewed August 28, 1972.
4. Ibid.

started to increase. Stover was an avid devotee of the chase, and over the years, he had developed the skills and knowledge any good nimrod needs to insure that he gets his buck every year.

One proven technique the old hunter used for increasing his chance of seeing that nice big eight or ten point was to keep the salt lick he had set up in the foot hills below Paddy Mountain in Penn Township well stocked with a big block of salt. Deer were attracted to this rare treat, and Stover often laid in wait nearby so he could "pot" the biggest bucks as they savored the saline taste of the salt blocks.

Once in a while, if there happened to be more than one trophy buck that wandered into the salt lick in any given year, it mattered not to Stover; he would shoot them all. Like many of the old hunters who had hunted in the days before game laws were introduced, Stover's hunting ethics were still rooted in the past, and so he was not hesitant about shooting does or bucks at any time of the year, whether it was deer season or not.

The old hunter must have had quite a collection of magnificent antlers displayed in his house, the result of his many years of harvesting deer whenever they crossed his path, but there was one set of horns that was absent from his fine display and which he wished he had. This missing set may have even diminished the pleasure he got from admiring all the others that hung in profusion on his walls, for the missing antlers would have been from the buck that got away, the one that fought back.

The story of Stover's fighting stag began one day when the cagey hunter was treed near his salt lick. He had climbed up to a deer stand fastened in a tree above the lick, and he sat there silently, perhaps contemplating his chances of bringing down a buck with the biggest antlers anyone had ever seen. But then his reveries were broken when a large buck wandered into the clearing below. Although probably not nearly as big as the one that Stover may have been hoping for, he shot it anyway and, thinking he had killed it, came down out of the tree to "dress" his trophy.

As Stover began the bloody work of gutting the fallen buck, it suddenly revived, and after fully recovering its senses, it stood up. It shook itself, and then its natural survival instincts took over from there. Much to the hunter's chagrin, the "dead" deer became an enraged blur of horns and hide, which began chasing him around the tree where the deer stand was located.

It was an even race for a while, but Stover began to lose speed as he ran out of wind, and the stag managed to gore the frightened hunter in the leg several times with its horns. His injuries would have been much worse if the little cur he had with him hadn't begun to bark in a high-pitched frenzy.

Despite its puny size, the little dog's yips unnerved the buck, and the noise scared it away. Too surprised and exhausted to pursue his "dead" buck, Stover decided to call it a day, and he never caught the stag, but his descendants say that he "carried the scars of that deer's horns for the rest of his life."[5]

There was yet another Centre County hunter whose fight with a buck was even more desperate than Jackson Stover's. In this case, the hunter, like Stover, had his dog along with him, too, and that once again proved to be a stroke of luck. John Lingle's encounter occurred over the mountains lying to the south of Coburn during a time described by our storyteller as "years ago when deer weren't very plentiful."

"Now I heard John Lingle, he was an old man at the time, tell that they were out hunting, and they only had these muzzleloaders that fired one shot,"[6] began the former resident of Poe Valley. The nearby lumbering town of Poe Paddy is now only a memory, but every year, the wondrously wild Poe Paddy and Poe Valley State Parks that have been sensibly preserved by the Commonwealth perpetuate the memory of that once-thriving village.

Every year, the parks and their hundreds of acres of surrounding state forest land attract hundreds of visitors seeking their solitude and natural charms, but few visitors are aware of the interesting stories that could once be heard about this region, including the story of John Lingle's unusual fight with a deer.

"Well, they were in Poe Valley, and they chased these deer from Little Poe Mountain down to Big Poe Mountain," continued the valley native who had once known John Lingle personally. "Now, this is true. They heard shots, but they didn't know right which way. Then, pretty soon, he heard a dog barking. So by and by, now this was old John Lingle; he heard a deer coming closer. It was a buck, a big one, and he shot at it but only

---

5. Blaine Malone (born 1903), interviewed October 23, 1980 and April 21, 1981.
6. Clayton Auman (born 1885), recorded October 31, 1981.

crippled it. The deer then went for him, and he grabbed its horns, one with each hand, but it pinched him in there.

"The deer tried to get him against a tree, but with his hands, he turned it around the tree. Now, this is no lie! Old John Lingle told me this often. And he said they were coming down the mountain like hell; the dog, too. But finally the dog caught them, you know, and the dog jumped up and got the deer by the throat and choked it. Now, this is no hot story. Well, then he shot him, too."[7]

Anyone who thinks the preceding tales are indeed just "hot" stories made up by a hunter trying to impress his hunting camp compatriots should not pass judgment until they've done at least one of three things: Spend enough time in the great outdoors to actually get to know the habits of deer, read

Every hunter's dream. Not many big bucks with horns like this are seen in the Pennsylvania mountains today!

the autobiographies of the old time Pennsylvania hunters like Philip Tome and Meshach Browning, or talk to some present-day hunters and listen to their stories of the mountains. These tales of the chase will no doubt cause doubters to change their minds.

There is no doubt that bucks will charge a person given the right conditions. Does will, too, as anyone who has gotten too close to a doe that is with newborn fawn can attest, and this writer can be included in that number. In fact, records of several such encounters with the male of the species have been preserved in various historical texts that document the natural history of the state.

Histories of Clinton County, for example, tell of "a citizen who once owned the lands on which Renovo now stands" being charged by a sizeable buck. The account also goes on to state that the citizen would probably have been gored to death except for the fact that the beams of the horns were so far apart that the man could squeeze himself between them and

7. Ibid.

hold on "so as to not allow the prongs to enter his body." In this case, the man "was relieved by the timely arrival of another hunter, who dispatched the buck and rescued him from certain death!"[8]

The same historical records of Clinton County preserve yet another interesting deer-attacks-man episode that is said to have occurred near Young Womanstown, now North Bend, in Chapman Township. Here, one day, a farmer's pack of dogs chased and managed to corner a nice buck. However, the snarling and barking mongrels could not subdue the stag, and, in an attempt to assist them, a farmhand tried to do so. His efforts were rewarded by a strong thrust of the buck's horns, which caught him in his hand. It was a painful lesson and one which "disabled him for several weeks."[9]

So, it obviously becomes safe to say that the stories of hunters' hand-to-horn clashes with deer do include dogs at times, and Philip Tome, the legendary nimrod of the West Branch Valley and northwestern Pennsylvania, would have had some definite idea of which breed was best suited to have along in any hand-to-hand, or, more accurately, hand-to-antler duel with a deer.

Tome's fascinating book entitled *Pioneer Life, or Thirty years a Hunter*, preserves his many recollections of the days when he was an interpreter for Seneca chiefs Cornplanter and Blacksnake, and it also contains his recollections of the times when he stalked elk, panthers, wolves, and deer in Lycoming, Warren, Potter, and Tioga Counties. His advice to other would-be nimrods was that to be a successful deer hunter, a person "should always procure at any cost the largest and best dogs to be found," with the best breed, in his opinion being "half bloodhound, a quarter cur, and the other quarter greyhound."[10]

Dogs would, of course, give a serious deer hunter a decided edge, but even then, there is always element of risk. However, despite the dangers that are inherent in deer hunting, there can also be a humorous side. Even Sam Askey, the great big game hunter of the Bald Eagle Valley in Centre County, was fond of recalling some of his lighter deer hunting moments

---

8. John Blair Linn, *History of Centre and Clinton Counties*, 585.
9. Philip Tome, *Pioneer Life, or Thirty Years a Hunter*, 107.
10. Ibid.

when regaling interested parties with many of his other daring accounts, episodes which one of his biographers described as "hairbreadth escapes from the denizens of the forest."[11]

Askey, who was born in 1776, must have kept his audience spellbound with his storytelling since his hunting escapades stretched back to the early 1800s when the mountains of Pennsylvania were a hunter's paradise. The veteran hunter had his favorite hunting spots in that arboreal utopia, and one he liked the most was along the old Indian path leading from the Bald Eagle Valley into the small town of Snow Shoe. Known as the Bald Eagle Path, the trail was named after the same local Indian chief whose name rests upon the valley today.

It was along this path that Askey had what he would later describe as "an amusing and ridiculous scrape"[12] with a large buck he spotted one day while out hunting. The buck was quite a distance away when he first saw it, but Askey decided to take the long shot anyway. His aim was true; when the rifle cracked, the deer went down "flat in his tracks."[13]

Thinking he had made a "dead shot," Askey pulled out his hunting knife with his right hand and walked up to the stag. The veteran hunter bent down and grabbed one of the buck's antlers with his left hand and then started to apply the knife to the buck's throat.

Suddenly, and much to Askey's "utter dismay and astonishment," the buck violently jumped up, one of its horns going through part of the over-sized shirt that Askey was wearing. "He then gave me a tremendous whirl," recalled the hunter, "and in doing so, he relieved me of the blouse and departed!"

Askey was left standing in his shirtsleeves, relieved to be alive but amused by the sight of the blouse furling out from the buck's antlers "like the flag of a conquering hero" as the animal sped away. In later years, when asked if he resented the deer for stealing his shirt, Askey would always reply that he did not, noting, "If I had not been relieved of it, the results would have been much more serious."[14]

---

11. Dave Poust (born 1930), recorded February 27, 1998.
12. Ibid.
13. Ibid.
14. Ibid.

Despite the historical evidence, deer stories like Sam Askey's, John Lingle's, Jackson Stover's, and similar tales of other hunters might still seem far-fetched to those who have never heard these tales of the mountains before. People somehow expect such tales to be exaggerated since fishermen and hunters have been known to embellish the size of their trophies. Moreover, authors like Henry Shoemaker have added their embellishments to a factual episode now and then and, in doing so, made the authenticity of the entire tale suspect.

One example like this might be the deer encounter mentioned in the chapter titled "Hairy John," story VI in this volume. The story of the hog-tied deer waking up and running around the cabin sounds like a touch from the facile pen of Henry Shoemaker, but the episode has become woven into the tapestry of Penn's Valley legend and may have been based on real events after all.

Certainly, deer can sometimes fight back when desperate, and just in case anyone needs further proof of that fact, the following tale from Clinton County that occurred in the early 1970s is offered for the reader's consideration. The incident took place on Short Mountain in the Pine Creek Valley. The area is part of the main chain of the Allegheny Mountains that lies next to Tiadaghton State Forest near Waterville, the gateway to the Pine Creek Gorge and Pennsylvania's Grand Canyon country.

"The one I shot was when I was on a drive, up in Painter Hollow,"[15] said Dave Poust, the internationally awarded taxidermist at Waterville. Poust entertained us with many interesting hunting and fishing tales when we visited his taxidermy shop during the springtime of 1998, and this tale proved to be one of the funniest.

"It went to jump the run, and all I got was a shot from the hip. I never got the rifle up. I just took a shot when it was jumping the run. Well, I never figured I'd touched him. He was up there about eighty yards, and I went up, and there he laid in the run! Oh boy, big surprise here, you know. I got him!

"I almost kept right on goin' with the drive. There was an old loggin' trail right up from the bank, and I thought, 'Well, I'll just pull him up outa here and put him on that trail, and then when the drive's over, I'll come back down and drag him down the main road. I could see he was hit here

---

15. Dave Poust (born 1930), recorded February 27, 1998.

in the neck. There was blood on the neck, and I thought, 'Boy, that was a nice shot!'

"Well, anyway, I put the draggin' rope on him and started to pull him up over the bank, and all at once, he's on all four feet! He didn't like bein' led around! Well, him and I went around and around in the 'crick' bottom; it's all loose stone and everything, and it was just clangin' and bangin'. I'd set my gun up on the top of the bank first while I got my draggin' rope out, but I had him by the end of the rope, and he had me!

"I finally got to a little white pine tree about a little bigger than a broom stick, and I got the rope tied around it. Well, now he's backin' up, and he's shakin' his head; it was a big seven point. Nice buck! The other driver that was above me heard all this clangin' and bangin', and he hollered down, 'What's goin' on?'

"I said, 'Come on down!' and he come down. I said, 'This one big enough or do you want me to get a bigger one? I don't know whether to shoot it or let it go!

"He said, 'I never seen anything like this!'

'Well,' I said, 'If you think it's a keeper, I'll keep it!'

"Here, that bullet had just creased the back of the neck, right back of the ears. It never hit the spinal cord or anything. What it did, it knocked it out; the shock through the spinal cord knocked it out. If I'd've kept right on goin' after I shot it, when I come back, I'd've sworn somebody stole that deer!"[16]

At the risk of belaboring the point, there are a few Potter County tales of a hunter's hand-to-horn combat with an enraged buck that I'd like to share as well. They not only support the idea that such encounters did happen but also show just how rough and ready the old-time hunters once were.

In the history of Potter County, it is noted that "It has been held by many that a deer cannot be held by a man, and we really think it a very dangerous undertaking to attempt it."[17] The author then goes on to share several anecdotes to show that some disregarded that cautionary warning.

---

16. Ibid.

17. J. H. Beers and Company, *History of the Counties of McKean, Elk, Cameron, and Potter, Pennsylvania*, 1000-1003.

One such incident occurred in Hector Township of Potter County in the late nineteenth century when a hunter was following a deer trail covered by "noisy" snow (a snowfall crusted under a freezing rain). The track led up a steep mountainside and through a laurel thicket. Skirting the thicket, he hid behind a tree on the other side and waited for the deer to come out.

Once it appeared, he jumped upon its back and wrestled it to the ground like a rodeo steer wrestler. At that moment, the deer was able to send him flying with a violent kick of its rear legs, which completely tore the man's clothes from his body and allowed the deer to run away.[18]

Somewhat a glutton for punishment, this same hunter, at a later time, shot a buck and trailed it until he found it lying behind a log, apparently dead. Just as he reached over the log and grabbed its antlers so he could start dressing it, the buck jumped up and charged him. The hunter was able to move behind a small tree for protection and still managed to hold onto the buck's antlers.

The struggle continued for hours, with the hunter hoping that the deer would eventually wear out due to loss of blood. The deer did not show signs of fatigue, even appearing to grow stronger as time went on. Finally, realizing his strength was ebbing, the hunter began calling for help. Two other hunters walking along a nearby road heard his cries and came to his rescue. The men later "claimed that had they not happened along as they did, the deer would have killed our friend."[19]

One final Potter County episode ends on a happier note for the deer that was involved. It's a story that was said to have made the hunter involved "famous all over Potter County."[20] In this case, the nimrod, Ephraim Bishop, also followed a snow-covered deer trail to a Spicewood thicket, where the deer had concealed themselves.

Bishop loosed his deer hound to force the deer from the thicket, and the animals scattered far and wide. Not to be thwarted, he picked up their trail, circling three times around a path that was five miles in circumference. After four hours of pursuit, the hunter found one deer hiding in the deepest part of a brush pile along the section known as the old King Road.

---

18. Ibid.
19. Ibid.
20. Ibid.

Without hesitation, Bishop leaped upon it and, after tiring it, tied a string he had in his pocket around its neck and to a tree. Then, after obtaining a logging sled, he was able to load the deer onto it and transport it back to a neighbor's barn, later selling it as payment for a debt he owed to a gentleman who wanted to display it a county fairs and carnivals.[21]

21. Ibid.

CHAPTER 16

INDIAN SUMMER

Etymologists today now recognize that the term "American Indian" is not a self-applied descriptor originating from today's Native American cultures. Likewise the term "Indian" is considered to be an import from European languages from the time of Christopher Columbus. However, this theory also is subject to some debate.

In 1492, Columbus was dispatched by Spanish monarchs Ferdinand and Isabella with a passport stating that he was to sail "toward regions of India." Europeans had long been interested in finding an ocean route to the riches of Southeast Asia, explored overland via the Silk Road by Marco Polo in prior centuries. These spices, dyes, fabrics, gems, and precious metals traveled overland routes and were thought to originate in India, China, Japan, and the Spice Islands (aka Indies/Indonesia). Thus, when Columbus mistakenly dubbed the Caribbean natives he first contacted "Indians," he thought he might be in the Indies or near India.

Then, in the last half of the twentieth century, the term "Indian" was replaced by "Native American," which was considered more politically correct and less pejorative. However, that newer term, now in widespread use, has still only been partially accepted by indigenous cultures. Consisting of many different tribal units with each one having a unique name, the members of those affiliations prefer to be referred to by their affiliation name. Likewise, the descriptor "American Indian" is also considered to be of non-indigenous origins and a pejorative term, particularly when used in phrases like "the Indian Wars" of Colonial times.

Schoch's Block House. Replica of a typical pioneer refuge that was a welcome haven for settlers when the Indians renewed their frontier raids on warm "Indian Summer" days. This one once stood along Route 522 near the village of Kreamer in Snyder County, but the last time I passed by I found only an historical marker here; the block house was no longer there. The original it was modeled after was built on Matthias Schoch's Tract around 1770 and used during the Revolutionary War and up until 1783.

The term "Indian Wars" was a phrase widely used by historians to refer to conflicts that occurred during the times of the French and Indian War of the 1750s and of the Revolutionary War of the 1770s. However, in both cases, they were fought by colonists and European powers, with indigenous peoples squeezed between two nations competing for sovereignty over lands the natives considered to be their own.

Forced to choose sides in those conflicts, the Indians, decimated by European-imported pestilences, weakened by their own internal strife, confronted by superior weaponry, and overwhelmed by a lack of understanding of the European concept of land ownership, lost control of their lands, but not without a fight.

People on the frontier lived in fear during those terrible times: fear of furtive Indian raids led by notorious Indian war chiefs like Shingas,

Captain Jacobs, and Hiokoto, and fear of ending up victims of those raids, like so many of their contemporaries.

Scalped and dying neighbors were gruesome reminders of the hazards of frontier life, and a night sky reddened by burning settlements over the mountains was another such reminder for the inhabitants of Northumberland County in 1778 and of Lehigh County in 1755.

Gradually, the peace-loving Quakers who comprised the Provincial Government in Philadelphia realized they couldn't disregard the plight of the frontiersmen any longer. The Scotch-Irish and German settlers needed a means of defense, and so, with great reluctance, the Quakers authorized the construction of a chain of forts that played a key role in the bloody Indian wars that were to follow. These bastions, structures the Indians would later refer to as "strong houses,"[1] proved to be so effective that they at last provided the relief the settlers living on the frontier had prayed for. Eventually, the frontier forts became such a normal part of the frontier experience that the word "fort" was used as both a noun and a verb.[2]

Raids on pioneer settlements by Indian marauders were always possible during Pennsylvania's frontier days, and no one knew for sure when the sound of the war-whoop would be heard in the forest. However, summer was the usual time when roving bands of warriors set out on their bloody mission, and only the most foolhardy or fearless settlers refused to fort during those peak periods when reports of Indian hostilities got too close for comfort. The sturdy log bastions must have looked very inviting during these times of terror, but like almost everything else, there were advantages and disadvantages to living within the relatively safe walls of a frontier fortress.

Inconvenience and discomfort were two of the drawbacks associated with the forting experience; loss of privacy was yet another. Being confined in tight quarters with one's neighbors for weeks on end must have been nerve-wracking for independent settlers who loved the isolation of the frontier, but confinement also fostered a sense of cooperation. The natural rhythm of the seasons did not stop just because people were holed up in a fort, and so there was still livestock to feed and crops to tend.

1. C. Hale Sipe, *The Indian Wars of Pennsylvania*, 152.
2. J. F. Meginness, *Otzinachson*, 506; *and* Thomas Lynch Montgomery, *Frontier Forts of Pennsylvania, Volume 2*, 418.

Determined to keep their farms productive even during the times when they were forted, the frontier agriculturalists, drawn to their fields, would occasionally band together and leave the protection of the fortress. Groups of men, their muskets on their shoulders, would make their way back to their clearings and help one another in their respective fields.

But despite the need for as many helping hands as they could get, the fearless farmers always chose one of their number as a sentry to watch for Indians. With the sentry on guard, the others would stack their muskets in a convenient spot and then begin their labors in earnest. Nonetheless, despite their precautions, settlers like these, with their loaded muskets nearby, were still sometimes killed or captured as they toiled together in their fields.

Given the difficulties of life both inside and outside a fort during times of Indian attack, it is no wonder that frontier families were glad to return to their homes when the danger had passed or when the first frosts coated the leaves of sturdy oaks and settled on maples tinged with the first colors of fall. Although their homes were nothing more than crude cabins, they must have felt like castles after the stresses of forting.

Even today many of us have pleasant mental pictures of these frontier homesteads surrounded by wide open spaces and verdant forests, but life in those early cabins could be very different than the romantic images we see in our mind's eye today.

"This house looks and smells like a shambles," wrote Reverend Philip Fithian in his journal in 1775. The itinerant minister had been invited to stay a while with a Centre County settler and his family, but the preacher was totally unprepared for the lifestyle of a typical frontiersman.

Although he was grateful for shelter, Fithian was appalled by a house he described as being filled with "raw flesh and blood, fish and deer, flesh and blood in every part, mangled wasting flesh on every shelf. Hounds licking up the blood from the floor; an openhearted landlady; naked Indians and children; ten hundred thousand flies," and he feared "as many fleas." It was not a lifestyle for a person used to more refined surroundings like Fithian, and so he concluded, "I would not live here for five hundred a year!"[3]

---

3. John Blair Linn, *History of Centre and Clinton Counties*, 16.

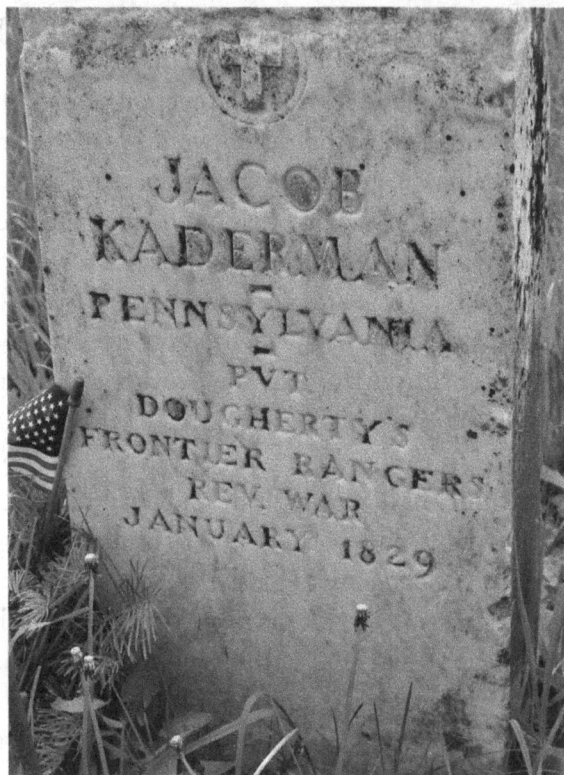

An interesting reminder of Pennsylvania's Indian Days.
This historical remnant can be found in a remote patriot
cemetery on a hillside along Red Ridge Road near
Mifflinburg, Union County.

The Indians Fithian mentioned in his journal were friendly ones, but many in those times were not. It is from this fact that still another term arose from the frontier experience: the term Indian Summer. It is a phrase that conjures up pleasant thoughts for us today, but once again, the reality that formed the basis for the expression is far different from our romanticized concepts.

The mention of Indian Summer was cause for alarm in the minds of the state's early settlers, according to Joseph Doddridge, that early chronicler of western Pennsylvania's Indian wars.[4] Although the first signs of frost meant that Indian war parties would be heading back to their homes in the north for the winter, there was always the chance that the icy gusts of

---

4. C. Hale Sipe, *The Indian Chiefs of Pennsylvania*, 13.

November would be broken by a string of balmy days when a smoke-like haze covers the land.

It was sometimes during those days that Indian warriors would decide they had time for one more raid before the bone-chilling days of winter arrived at last. The name Indian summer was the title the early settlers gave to this season, and it turned out to be so appropriate that it became a part of the folklore of the frontier.

Although the expression is rooted in terror, it is such a powerfully attractive one that we still use it today. Perhaps the reason for that is because it reminds us of a time and place that seems better than it really was, or perhaps we find it appealing because it preserves a memory of a race of people that we wronged, and we feel a need to rectify that injustice.

Either way, the expression does evoke images of a vanished people, and so it seemed fitting to discuss its origins in this little essay in order to lay the foundation for two tales that preserve a memory of how the state's Indians eventually became reluctant participants in the European colonists' culture. The first of these two stories might be called "The Tale of the Sputtering Candles," and the second, "A Full-blooded Indian."

The tale of the spluttering candles occurred in a secluded vale of the Bald Eagle Mountains near Port Matilda, Centre County, where Laurel Run winds its way down to Bald Eagle Creek. Passersby through here may have seen the highway marker that notes Reese Hollow Road, just off Route 220 and near the little town whose name poses a bit of a mystery to those who study the origins of such things. On the other hand, although the source of Port Matilda's name has been lost over time, the origin of the name of Reese Hollow is well known to the descendants of John Christian Reese.

"He was a Hessian soldier, brought over to fight, to put down the uprising of the colonies for King George of England," recalled one of Reese's proud descendants. "He got captured at Trenton, New Jersey when George Washington crossed the Delaware, and then he served two hitches in the navy for Washington. But it was his granddaughter, my great-grandmother, that told this story; I think my mother told it to me. My mother was raised by her grandmother instead of her mother, so it was almost like her mother.

"My great-grandmother's name was Delilah. I couldn't tell you when she was born, but my mother was born in 1898. When my great-grandmother went to housekeeping, she went to housekeeping in a log house, probably with a dirt floor, up in Reese Hollow. There might yet be stones there from the foundation, but later on they built a regular house on the same site, and it still stands today.

John Christian Reese had this whole hollow, and he was a millwright with a sawmill there at Laurel Run. They didn't have money to pay for the land, but some way or other, he got it; I don't know, maybe from the war or something."[5] [Author's Note: The Colonial government didn't have any money either, and so they often paid the veterans of the Revolutionary War with land grants].

It was here in their homestead, in the hollow that today still bears their name, that the last remaining Indians of the area often visited the Reeses. The unexpected visits usually took place without incident, but during one particular time, something so unusual happened that it became part of the Reese family's oral history and remains so today.

"It was late in the evening, and the Indians came in to get milk for their babies," recalled the man who had heard the tale from his mother. "They would usually give them milk if they had extra. This one evening, the Indians happened by; they wouldn't come regular, I guess, and the men were either out hunting or away some place.

"But the women and children were there, and my great-grandmother was one of them. And the Indians come in to get milk for their babies. They'd always give 'em the best they could, but they was always afraid what they'd do when the men wasn't there. And this night, the men wasn't there, and the women were a little skeptical about what the Indians would be up to.

"But anyway, they had candlelight in those days; it was what they used to see by. And the way they made the candles was to dip the wicks in tallow, and then they'd put it over into water to cool it, and back and forth until they got the candle big enough. On this night, when the Indians came, the candles were burning, and it got down to where there must have been some water in them, and the candles started to spit and sputter. The sounds scared the Indians, and they took off without even taking the milk for their babies. The women was much relieved; they didn't know what the Indians would do!"[6]

---

5. John Blazosky (born 1926), recorded October 18, 1996.
6. Ibid.

Another Patriot gravestone and a link to the Indian wars. Also to be found in the remote patriot cemetery on a hillside along Red Ridge Road near Mifflinburg, Union County.

The second episode that recalls the manner in which Indians may have gradually learned the white man's ways is a humorous story that once circulated in or around Johnstown, Cambria County, about 1890 to 1900. The anecdote may be based on a real incident, or at the very least, a real Indian, but at this late date, there is no way to know for sure.

However, there are perhaps some elements to the story that convey a picture of just how completely many Pennsylvania Indians became assimilated into American society. Whether that assimilation was good or bad can be the subject of lengthy discussions, but there is little doubt that how it all took place is not something that we should look back upon today with a sense of satisfaction or pride.

"The only Indian I ever saw was Sammy Sanook; he was educated at the Carlisle Indian School,"[7] recalled the former native of Johnstown, who proved to be an invaluable link to the past. The grand old man had helped with the cleanup of the city after Johnstown was devastated by the infamous

7. Abraham Lincoln Maurer (born 1872), interviewed May 25, 1974.

The Indians' Twilight. A nostalgic depiction of how Pennsylvania's Native Americans faded into obscurity. (Drawing by James J. Frazier.)

flood of May 31, 1889, and he was two years past the century mark when he sat down with me and talked of the old days.

Stories of wolves, ghosts, and Indians were still common when he was a young man, and his recollection of the Carlisle Indian reminded him of a joke he'd heard when he was fifteen to twenty years old: a joke about a different Indian who lived "somewhere up around Johnstown.

"This Indian had to pass through town to get to his cabin," continued the man, who was born in the first few years following the end of the Civil War, "and on this one day when he was passing through, he saw a blood bank set up there. He spoke good English and so knew what a sand bank was and an ore bank, but this 'bank' was new to him. So he asked someone, 'Whose blood are they taking now?'

"They persuaded him to go have a look and so he did. The nurse there tried to get him to donate, but he was scared. She explained it all to him and showed him that none of the donors had been hurt. So the Indian finally gave a pint and sat down to rest. Three donors finally noticed him sitting there and, since Indians were scarce, asked him if he was a full-blooded Indian. 'Yes,' he said, 'short one pint!'[8]

Today, in Pennsylvania's cities there are no easily identified lone Indians that can be singled out as a living reminder of the once-proud and powerful

---

8. Ibid.

race that at one time lived on this very same soil and hunted in the forests that covered it. It is a sad fact, but the verdant land of the Indians has too often been replaced with development and landscaping.

Where there were once forests and fields, there are now housing developments, parking lots, factories, and shopping centers that no one wants or which cannot find businesses to rent their retail spaces. Nonetheless, despite what sometimes seems to be our best efforts, there will always be some things we cannot take away from Native Americans: the names that they gave to Pennsylvania's mountains, rivers, valleys, streams, and their towns, from which come the names of some of our cities and towns.

Perhaps the words of the poet say it best, and in a way, the Indians may have said it themselves:

"Ye say they have all pass'd away,
That noble race and brave,
That their light canoes have vanish'd,
From off the crested wave;

That 'mid the forest where they roam'd,
There rings no hunter's shout;
But their name is on your waters;
Ye may not wash it out.

Ye say their cone-like cabins,
That cluster'd o'er the vale
Have disappear'd as wither'd leaves,
Before the autumn gale;

But their memory liveth on your hills,
Their baptism on your shore,
Your everlasting rivers speak,
Their dialect of yore."[9]

---

9. Lydia Huntley Sigourney, "Indian Names"; Rufus W. Griswold, *Readings in American Poetry*, 59.

Conrad Weiser's Gravesite. Located at the Conrad Weiser Homestead historical site in Womelsdorf, Berks County, this was the burial place of one the most important figures in Pennsylvania's colonial history. As Indian agent for the Penn family, he negotiated many treaties with the Indians, and treated them so fairly and with such respect that many of their chiefs wished to be buried next to him when they died. They lie there today beside him in unmarked graves.

/

CHAPTER 17

GYPSY CARAVANS

When deciding which tales rank among the most fascinating annals of Pennsylvania's legendary lore, the stories of that unique race of people known as Gypsies must certainly be considered as prime candidates. The old-timers who remember them recall the unusual lifestyle of the Gypsies, but most often, they remember their caravans of gaudily painted horse-drawn wagons that could sometimes be seen winding their way along the back roads and over the Pennsylvania mountains as late as the first decades of the twentieth century. Known all over the world as wanderers, Gypsies have always been content to live on the fringes of society, taking on occupations that fit in with their mobile lifestyles.

In Europe they were often employed in part-time and seasonal work, and they also served as dogcatchers, hangmen, undertakers, and in other similar jobs that no one else really wanted to do. Generally, however, the Gypsy men were known for their talents as musicians, blacksmiths, and horse dealers. Gypsy women, on the other hand, earned money by providing services that a local populace would never consider supplying, unique things such as fortunetelling and theatrical entertainment. Nonetheless, despite their honest endeavors, the Gypsies were also known for their dishonesty.

They had a reputation for thievery and trickery, and since they seemed to disdain normal societal structures and were strangers wherever they went, they were always treated as outcasts. People not only mistrusted Gypsies because of their strange lifestyle and unsavory reputations but also

Romani with their wagon. Typical of what their wagons looked like when Gypsy caravans could once be seen winding their way over Pennsylvania's high mountain roads and through the towns in the valleys below. This photo was taken in the Rhineland of Germany in 1935. (Credit: Bundesarchiv, Bild 183-J0525-0500-003 / CC-BY-SA Creative Commons License - German Federal Archives.)

because they were not locals. They had no roots, and no one knew where they came from. In Europe, they called themselves "Rom," which, when translated from their own tongue, merely means "man," but the early German settlers here in Pennsylvania preferred instead to call them *Zigeuner*, meaning "vagrants," while "Black Dutch" was the appellation preferred by the Gypsies once they had settled in the Pennsylvania Dutch regions.[1]

English settlers thought that since the word Gypsy was probably derived from the word Egyptian then Gypsies must have originated in that country, but those who have studied the matter say their country of origin was India. Their typically dark complexions, jet-black hair, and bright, gaudy clothes could be evidence showing a connection to India, but these things also made them stand out.

Moreover, Gypsy women could sometimes be strikingly beautiful, and they accentuated this beauty by wearing large pieces of colorful ornamental

1. Https://smithsonianeducation.org/gyp.

And yet another. I recall seeing Gypsies at County Fairs when I was a teenager. They were recognizable from their garish clothes and makeup, their fancy jewelry, and their darker complexions. Even then the common advice was to avoid them due to their shady reputations!

jewelry. Wherever they went, the flamboyant Gypsies were noticed, and although they were undoubtedly sometimes the culprits, they were also often wrongly blamed for many misfortunes, thefts, and misdeeds that happened in farms, towns, and villages that they passed through, like the time the water turned to poison on Trimble Hill.

About halfway down the slope of Trimble Hill in Indiana County, there was once a watering trough. It was a favorite camping place for Gypsies since they could attract customers from the many travelers passing by here on the public road. People would stop to have their fortunes told or to see the roadside vagabonds perform, and the Gypsies' business boomed until local farmers began to complain about disruptions to wagon traffic.

Matters stood unchanged for a while until a few of the more disgruntled individuals decided to take matters in hand. So it was that one day, a band of gun-toting township men marched out to the Gypsy camp and ordered them to leave the area. The cheery vagrants seemed to accept their fate meekly enough, but later on, when horses drank water from the Trimble Hill watering trough, they became sick, and some died agonizing deaths.

People didn't have to think too long before concluding that the Gypsies
had put a curse upon the spring that supplied the water for the trough. It
was obvious to most that since the Gypsies could tell fortunes, they must
also know many of the other black arts, including ways to poison a perfectly
good water source. Others weren't so sure, but most local folks didn't give
the Gypsies the benefit of the doubt at all, and so the mysterious wayfarers
were tried and convicted *in absentia* by the powers of superstition.

Although the way in which the band of Gypsies was found guilty in
this case would not hold up in a court of law, it must still be said that Gypsies as a group were not very concerned about their reputations. They were
looked upon with suspicion by many of the reputable country folk, who,
themselves, were regarded as second-class citizens by some of the more
snobbish city dwellers.

Condescendingly referred to as "hill men," "clodhoppers," and "Busch
Deutsch"[2] by their city cousins, the upstanding inhabitants of rural
Pennsylvania during the last century must have sometimes wondered what
names their detractors used when referring to the Gypsies. Whatever the
names used to describe them, the Gypsies were certainly victims of prej-
udice. However, in this case, there were apparently many instances that
strengthened and validated those prejudices, just like an episode that took
place around 1920 near the quaint Centre County town of Woodward.

"When I was a kid, there were a lot of Gypsies, and a bunch used
to come here to this Woodward Cave and Campground area," recalled
the lifelong resident of that same section. "Of course, they were people
that you gotta watch. They made baskets; the women weaved baskets from
willows. There was a lot of willows up along here, and I think that's why
they parked in here.[3]

"Then the men would go out and sell these baskets during the daytime.
But they were also known as crooks and pickpockets, and I do know that
they actually did pickpocket Ray Stover, an old gentleman in Woodward.

"A man and a woman, Gypsy, came onto the porch and wanted to sell him
baskets, but he didn't want them. He told them, 'I've all the baskets I need,'
but they kept talking to him and talking to him, while in the meantime, the

2. Pennsylvania Writers Project, *Pennsylvania; A Guide to the Keystone State*, 64.
3. Ray Stover (born 1912), recorded May 19, 1989.

The old watering trough. It still sits along Route 144 near the top of Nittany Mountain, Centre County. A surviving relic of an earlier day when teamsters hauling tan bark and logs would stop here to water their horses when crossing the mountain.

lady got hold of his wallet some way. He never found it out 'til after they were gone; his wallet was missing, and he never did get it back!"[4]

Elderly folks living in other parts of the state could probably add their own stories about the thievery committed by Gypsies, just like some of

---

4. Ibid.

Closeup of the Nittany Mountain watering trough. A photo-shopped version to remove the obscene graffitti that was painted upon it. It perhaps is identical to the watering trough that once sat on Trimble Hill, Indiana County, that early settlers there thought had been poisoned by Gypsies.)

the older residents living in the shadow of Mount Riansares near the small Nittany Valley town of Mackeyville in Clinton County.

"Oh, Gypsies every summer,"[5] chortled ninety-three-year-old Cliff Vonada. Known for his infectious laugh and easy sense of humor, the old

_____

5. Cliff Vonada (born 1905), and wife Vera, recorded May 13, 1998.

farmer was the unofficial town historian, full of remembrances of the old days. Active and hearty his entire life, he drove a tractor and plowed all his own fields up until the year his legs finally "gave out." However, his mind remained as unclouded as it always was, and he relished the memories of his country life, including those of when the Gypsies used to camp along Fishing Creek in Mackeyville near where the local Kiwanis Club had built a medical center for local residents. He also recalls a day in the first few years of the 1920s when he was mowing hay with a team of horses, and these same Gypsies robbed a neighbor.

"They come through every place with their horses," stated Mr. Vonada in 1998. "The little lot that's growed up on this side of the Health Camp was vacant at one time, and Dr. Dunn left them in, and they camped there. All they did was camp and rest a while, but they could tell your fortune! Oh yeah, one would tell your fortune while the other was robbin' ya!

"They'd come out here, and I remember one time my dad was helpin' Mr. Sager up here—we neighbored. Farmers all went together and helped each other. I was a kid back then. Mr. Sager's old dad was right back there in his field, and these Gypsies come along and got after him. They took his pocketbook and everything. I saw this, and so I run, and I tell Dad, and they come down, and they caught 'em down here. They got back his pocketbook and the other stuff they had stolen."[6]

The tale seemed to have an odd ending despite the fact that the townspeople must have been furious over the attempted robbery. Their consensus seemed to be that it was more trouble than it was worth to try to retain the Gypsies and their horses until law enforcement officials arrived. None of the culprits were arrested; instead, said Mr. Vonada, they kinda "just let 'em go!"[7]

Gypsy thievery was apparently so common that whenever they were sighted, the alarm went out, with neighbors warning neighbors that the Gypsies were coming. In a 1974 article appearing in the *Doylestown Intelligencer*, Lester Trauch (born in 1906) recalled the Bucks County Gypsies of his childhood and their unsavory reputations.

6. Cliff Vonada (born 1905), and wife Vera, recorded May 13, 1998.
7. Ibid.

"I was maybe five or six and living at my parents' bakery in Bedminster. Four or five gypsy wagons would descend on the village. The men stayed on the wagons and drove the horses. The women and children jumped off and ran into Keller's store, the hotel, Hockman's butcher shop, into houses if the doors were open (they would demand that the woman go down into the cellar and bring up the finest jelly or jam she had, or they would put a curse on her and her family) and our bakery.

"They swarmed into the store. While one or two were 'bargaining' for bread or cakes, others with long, wide dresses and skirts opened up showcases and cookie boxes and emptied the contents into their skirts, which they used as baskets.

"Neighbors and farmers telephoned one another ahead of the advancing gypsies. The men could lasso a chicken with their long whips, and someone would jump off the wagon and pick it up and steal it. They would also pick up pigs, geese or anything small enough.

Ending on a positive note, Trauch concluded, "They are perhaps the freest of free men. They have many admirable traits; they will not steal from each other. 'Always help brothers; never harm brothers; always pay when you owe although not necessarily in money; never be afraid,' sums up their philosophy."[8]

Gypsies are not as prevalent today, or at least not as obvious, as they once were. Forty-five years ago, they could still be easily picked out at county fairs, but they don't even seem to attend them anymore—at least you don't notice them. Perhaps they've just learned to blend so well into the fabric of modern times that they are unrecognizable from anyone else. On the other hand, maybe there aren't any Gypsies left after all, the Gypsy of old having faded away into the colors and mists of the past. If so, it would mean that the wish of a World War I doughboy no longer has any meaning.

Joyce Kilmer, the American poet who became famous for his poem entitled "Trees," was killed in France in 1918 during the Great War. One of the wishes he had expressed in a letter to his mother was that if he ever owned a piece of woodland, he would erect a sign on it saying that Gypsies would be welcome to camp there.

8. Jean Rollo, "History Lives: Gypsies," article appearing in the *Bucks County Herald*, Doylestown, PA, October 4, 2023.

A typical Gypsy camp. Picture on an old postcard with the caption "This postcard offers a rare glimpse of the presence of the Romani in Pennsylvania". Found in Pennsylvania Heritage Magazine, Spring 2017.

When the state of Pennsylvania set aside twenty-one acres of Bald Eagle State Forest, on Paddy Mountain in Union County, for a Joyce Kilmer State Forest Monument, they erected a sign at the entrance. The words on the sign, "Gypsies are welcome to camp here," would have pleased the World War I poet. But the sign, as well as the Gypsies it once beckoned, now seems to be gone, a missing part of Pennsylvania's colorful heritage.

NOTE: Apparently, Gypsies have not entirely disappeared after all. Now, their caravans are formed by gasoline-powered automobiles instead of colorful horse-drawn carriages, but their reputations have not changed. "They were around here the other summer," noted Mr. Vonada. "And they're still up to their old tricks, putting tar on roofs and driveways," chimed in his wife, alluding to the fact that the less-than-honest workmen did the job but used vastly inferior materials to do it. "Yeah," concluded Mr. Vonada, "They tell me you still gotta watch 'em!"[9]

---

9. Cliff Vonada (born 1905), and wife Vera, recorded May 13, 1998.

ACKNOWLEDGMENTS

(AND A PLEA FOR MORE STORIES)

Folktales of the "Good Old Days" cannot be preserved unless there are folks who remember them and who are, in turn, willing to share them. I've been fortunate to find many such people over the last fifty years, but others went "above and beyond" my pleas for stories. These are the people who are inspired as much as I am when hearing the episodes of a bygone age, and they are also the ones whose love for our mountains is as great as mine. It is this common bond, I feel, that has moved them to find others who can tell me more "fireside tales."

Among exceptional helpers like this would be Jim Maguire Jr. of *Restless Oaks* in McElhatten, who has spent many hours showing me around the mountains of Clinton County and who has put me in touch with some excellent storytellers there. Bill and Pat Tyson of Beech Creek in Clinton County also deserve a lot of thanks for their kind efforts and the time they spent uncovering tales and contacts.

All three of these Clinton Countians are dedicated to preserving the heritage of that area, and the results of the assistance they've given to me can be found in several episodes embedded in this volume's stories, including "Hand to Horn Combat" and "Gypsy Caravans." Likewise, future volumes in the Pennsylvania Fireside Tales series will contain still more tales that have been preserved as a direct result of help from the Tysons and Jim Maguire.

I would also like to thank my son James for all the illustrations used in this book and previous ones; his sketches always add a nice touch that seemingly brings the past to life even more than if they weren't included in the books. Thanks also must go to those readers who have taken the time to write or phone me with their own stories. Contacts like this are always a pleasant surprise and are greatly appreciated.

I'm always ready to pursue another lead, and so I would be delighted to hear from those who have an old-time tale similar to those found in these volumes. My current address is 100 Hawknest Way – Apt. 135, Bellefonte, Pa. 16823. Contact can also be made, and books ordered online (www. pafolktales.com). Thanks, and I hope to hear from you!

BIBLIOGRAPHY

Aldrich, Lewis Cass, *History of Clearfield County, Pennsylvania,* Syracuse, NY, D. Mason and Company, 1887.

Bayard, Samuel P., *Hill Country Tunes, Instrumental Folk Music of Southwestern Pennsylvania, Memoirs of the American Folklore Society #39,* Philadelphia, American Folklore Society, 1944.

Beers, J. H. & Co., *Commemorative Biographical Record of Central Pennsylvania, including the counties of Centre, Clinton, Union, and Snyder,* J. H. Beers & Co., Chicago, IL, 1898.

————. *History of the counties of McKean, Elk, Cameron, and Potter Pennsylvania,* J. H. Beers & Co., Chicago, IL, 1890.

Blackman, Emily C., *History of Susquehanna County, Pennsylvania,* Philadelphia, PA, Claxton, Remsen & Haffelfinger, 1873.

Brendle, Thomas R. & William S. Troxell, "Pennsylvania German Folk Tales, Legends, Once-Upon-A-Time Stories, Maxims, and Sayings," *Proceedings of the Pennsylvania German Society—Volume L.,* Norristown, PA, Pennsylvania German Society, 1944.

Coco, Gregory, *On the Bloodstained Field,* Gettysburg, PA, Thomas Publications, 1987.

Cornplanter, Jesse J., *Legends of the Longhouse,* Port Washington, NY, Ira J. Friedman, 1963.

Craft, Reverend David, *History of Bradford County Pennsylvania,* Philadelphia, PA, L. H. Everts, 1878.

Day, Sherman, *Historical Collections of the State of Pennsylvania,* Port Washington, NY, Ira J. Friedman, 1843, reprinted 1969.

Dyke, Samuel E., *The Pennsylvania Rifle,* Lancaster Country Bicentennial Committee, 1974.

Ecenbarger, William, "Penn's Sylvania," *APPRISE Magazine* (publication of WITF public television broadcasting), Hershey, PA, April 1989.

Faris, John T., *Seeing Pennsylvania,* Philadelphia, J. B. Lippincott, 1919.

Fiedel, Dorothy Burtz, *Ghosts and Other Mysteries,* Ephrata, PA, Science Press, 1997.

Fisher, Sydney G., *The Making of Pennsylvania,* Long Island, NY, Ira J. Friedman, Inc., 1896, reprinted 1969.

Fiske, John, *Myths and Myth-makers (Old Tales and Superstitions Interpreted by Comparative Mythology)*, Boston, MA, Houghton Mifflin & Co., 1893.

Fletcher, Stevenson W., *Pennsylvania Agriculture & Country Life, 1640-1840*, Harrisburg, Pennsylvania Historical & Museum Commission, 1971.

Glimm, James York, *Flatlanders and Ridgerunners*, Pittsburgh, University of Pittsburgh Press, 1983.

Griswold, Rufus W., *Readings in American Poetry*, John K. Riker, Philadelphia, 1843.

Harting, James E., *Extinct British Animals*, London, Trubner & Company, 1880.

Heckewelder, Reverend John, *History, Manner, & Customs of the Indian Nations*, Philadelphia, The Historical Society of Pennsylvania, 1876.

Henretta, J. E., *Kane and the Upper Allegheny*, Philadelphia, Winston & Co., 1929.

Heverly, Clement F., *History and Geography of Bradford County Pennsylvania*, Bradford, PA, Bradford County Historical Society, 1926.

Hohman, John G., *Pow-wows, or The Long Lost Friend (A collection of mysterious arts and remedies for man as well as animals)*, originally published in the United States in the first decades of the nineteenth century (approximately 1820)

Ingram, John H., *The Haunted Homes and Family Traditions of Great Britain*, Reeves and Turner Co., London, 1905.

Kerlin, William W., *Centre Hall, Centre County, Pennsylvania*, Centre Hall, PA, Centre Hall Fire Company, 1942.

Leckie, Robert, *The Wars of America*, New York, Harper and Row, 1968.

Lee, J. Marvin, "King of the Pennsylvania Forests," *Centre County Heritage, 1956-75*, Bellefonte, PA, Centre County Historical Society, 1975.

Linn, John Blair, *History of Centre and Clinton Counties, Pennsylvania*, Philadelphia PA, Louis H Everts Co., 1883.

Lloyd, Thomas W., *Ole Bull in Pennsylvania*, Altoona, PA, Tribune Press, 1921.

McKnight, William J., *Pioneer Outline History of Northwestern Pennsylvania*, Philadelphia, Lippincott Co., 1905.

Meginness, John F., *Otzinachson, A History of the West Branch Valley*, Williamsport, PA, Gazette Printing House, 1889.

Montgomery, Thomas L., editor, *Frontier Forts of Pennsylvania Volumes 1 & 2*, Harrisburg, PA, Pennsylvania Historical Commission, 1916.

Peck, George, D. D., *Wyoming; Its History, Stirring Incidents, and Romantic Adventures*, New York, Harper & Brothers, 1858.

Pennsylvania Writers Project, *Pennsylvania, A Guide to the Keystone State*, Philadelphia, University of Pennsylvania Press, 1940.

Potter County Historical Society authors, *Historical Sketches of Potter County*, Coudersport, PA, Potter County Historical Society, 1976.

Rung, Albert M., *Rung's Chronicles of Pennsylvania History*, Huntingdon, PA, Huntingdon County Historical Society, 1984.

Rupp, I. Daniel, *History of Lancaster County Pennsylvania*, Lancaster, PA, Gilbert Hills, 1844.

Schneck, Reverend B. S., *The Burning of Chambersburg Pennsylvania*, Philadelphia, Lindsay and Blakiston, 1864.

Sipe, C. Hale, *The Indian Chiefs of Pennsylvania*, Butler, PA, Ziegler Printing Co., 1927.

———, *The Indian Wars of Pennsylvania*, Harrisburg, The Telegraph Press, 1931.

Tantaquidgeon, Gladys, *Folk Medicine of the Delaware*, Harrisburg, Pennsylvania Historical Commission, 1972.

Tome, Phillip, *Pioneer Life, or Thirty Years a Hunter*, Baltimore, Gateway Press, 1854, reprinted 1989.

Wallace, Paul A. W., *Indians in Pennsylvania*, Harrisburg, Pennsylvania Historical Commission, 1970.

———, *Indian Paths of Pennsylvania*, Harrisburg, Pennsylvania Historical Commission, 1971.

Wilkinson, Norman B., *Ole Bull's New Norway, Historic Pennsylvania Leaflet #14*, Harrisburg, Pennsylvania Historical and Museum Commission, 1962.

ABOUT THE AUTHOR

JEFFREY R. FRAZIER is a native of Centre Hall, Centre County. A 1967 graduate of Penn State University with a BS degree in Science, he also holds an MBA in Finance from Rider University in New Jersey. He currently resides at 100 Hawknest Way, Graystone Court Villas–Apt. 135 Bellefonte, Pa., 16823. He can be reached via phone at 814-360-4401, or by email at jandhfra2@yahoo.com, or by contacting his publisher (Sunbury Press).

This Sunbury Press edition of Volume 3 of the author's Pennsylvania Fireside Tales series is a new edition and represents an expanded and improved version of all previous editions. Formatting has been improved, as well as the number and quality of photos, but all the same tales that appeared in the original editions are included in this edition, along with new details added in some cases that were obtained after the last edition was published.

www.ingramcontent.com/pod-product-compliance
Lightning Source LLC
Chambersburg PA
CBHW011159090426
42740CB00020B/3412